The Geopolitics of Deep Oceans

To Ruth

THE GEOPOLITICS OF DEEP OCEANS

John Hannigan

First published in 2016 by Polity Press

Polity Press
65 Bridge Street
Cambridge CB2 1UR, UK

Polity Press
350 Main Street
Malden, MA 02148, USA

ISBN-13: 978-0-7456-8018-7
ISBN-13: 978-0-7456-8019-4 (pb)

A catalogue record for this book is available from the British Library.

Library of Congress Cataloging-in-Publication Data

Hannigan, John A., 1948-
    The geopolitics of deep oceans / John Hannigan.
      pages cm
    Includes bibliographical references and index.
    ISBN 978-0-7456-8018-7 (hardback) – ISBN 978-0-7456-8019-4
(pbk.) 1. Ocean. 2. Abyssal zone. 3. Geopolitics. I. Title.
    JZ3690.H36 2015
    341.4'5–dc23
                                                                                      2015011653

Typeset in 10.5 on 12 pt Sabon
by Toppan Best-set Premedia Limited
Printed and bound in the UK by Clays Ltd, St Ives PLC

For further information on Polity, visit our website:
politybooks.com

Contents

Acknowledgements

In February 2015, a week ago as I write these lines, Eugenie Clark, the 'Shark Lady', died aged 92 at her home in Sarasota, Florida. In a lifetime filled with discovery, adventure and professional achievement, Eugenie made over 70 deep dives in submersibles, appeared in 50 television specials and documentaries, developed a shark repellent and discovered three species of fish new to science. One of the great pleasures of writing a book on deep oceans has been to come across a cast of larger than life characters like Eugenie Clark who collectively have contributed so much to our understanding of and fascination with the deep. Consider Arthur C. Clarke, the celebrated science fiction author, who was also a devoted diver and a tireless proselytizer for colonizing the underwater 'frontier' in the 1950s. And then there was the aristocratic Elisabeth Mann Borgese, daughter of the esteemed novelist Thomas Mann and member of the legendary Club of Rome, who probably did more than anyone to encourage the scholarly study of the Law of the Sea. And, of course, one should not forget Jacques Cousteau, inventor of the aqualung, captain of the research ship *Calypso*, underwater treasure hunter and pioneering marine ecological activist.

When I first floated the idea of writing about the geopolitics of deep oceans to Louise Knight, Senior Acquisitions Editor at Polity, it must have seemed somewhat of a leap of faith. While I had written books about environmental sociology and on the international politics of natural disasters, I had not published anything pertaining to oceans, except for a pair of journal articles on El Niños and meteorological science, and a piece decades ago on flag of convenience ships and maritime labour. To her everlasting credit, Louise believed in this project and sagely pointed me towards the excellent and related work being done by Klaus Dodds of Royal Holloway, University of London, and his colleagues on Polar Regions and critical geopolitics. Also at Polity, Louise's assistant Pascal Porcheron inherited the project from David Winters and has done a wonderful job shepherding it through the various stages of editorial review and production. Justin Dyer was a rigorous and perceptive copy-editor. At a point where I was just beginning to see how everything fitted together, Phil Burgess, Director of Policy and Research at the Global Ocean Commission, generously met with me at Somerville College, Oxford, to discuss the book project. It was reassuring to realize for the first time that I was headed in the right direction. I am indebted to one of the appraisers of this project (identified only as Reader #1), who went far beyond the call of duty in text-editing the manuscript as well as offering some really useful and collegial suggestions about books and articles I might want to read.

Finally, I could not have done this without the support of my family. When I was thinking about a new environmental writing project to follow *Disasters without Borders* (Hannigan, 2012), my wife Ruth and I talked at length about various possibilities – at one point volcanoes were a candidate – before I embraced her suggestion that I might want to consider oceans. Coming across the timely and suspenseful British television series *The Deep* sealed the deal. Ruth's love, interest and enthusiasm throughout this project have been vital to its success. Tim, our younger son, who starts his own professorial career at the University of Alberta in October 2015, assumed the critical task of merging the chapters into a single document. In addition, he offered up some insightful comments, as did TJ, his older brother, who is nearing completion of his doctorate at Temple University. The rest of the family, our two girls Maeve and Olivia and our 3½ year-old grandson Andrew, each provided support in their own way. Thank you one and all.

Abbreviations and Acronyms

ATOC	Acoustic Thermometry of Ocean Climate
ATS	Antarctic Treaty System
CBD	Convention on Biological Diversity
CCS	Carbon capture storage
CCZ	Clarion–Clipperton Zone
CHM	Common heritage of (hu)mankind
CLCS	UN Commission on the Limits of the Continental Shelf
COMRA	China Ocean Mineral Resources Research and Development Association
CSIRO	Commonwealth Scientific and Industrial Organization (Australia)
DARPA	Defense Advanced Research Projects Agency (US)
DNI	Directorate of Naval Intelligence (India)
DSDP	Deep Sea Drilling Project
ECSP	Extended Continental Shelf Project
EEZ	Exclusive Economic Zone
FAMOUS	French–American Mid-Ocean Undersea Study
HERMES	Hotspot Ecosystem Research on the Margins of European Seas
IDOE	International Decade of Ocean Exploration
IGO	Intergovernmental organization
IGY	International Geophysical Year
IOC	Intergovernmental Oceanographic Commission

IOI	International Ocean Institute
IPCC	Intergovernmental Panel on Climate Change
ISA	International Seabed Authority
IUCN	International Union for Conservation of Nature
JOGMEC	Japan Oil, Gas and Metals National Corporation
LFASs	Low-frequency active sonars
LOSC	United Nations Law of the Sea Convention
NASA	National Aeronautics and Space Administration
NGO	Non-governmental organization
NIEO	New International Economic Order
NOAA	National Oceanic and Atmospheric Administration
ONR	Office of Naval Research (US)
PDAC	Prospectors and Developers Association of Canada
PNG	Papua New Guinea
POGO	Partnership for Observation of Global Oceans
SCUBA	self-contained underwater breathing apparatus
UFP	Upward Falling Payloads
UNCLOS	United Nations Law of the Sea Conference
UNEP	United Nations Environment Programme
WHOI	Woods Hole Oceanographic Institution

Text Boxes

Note on Measurements

Whilst it is not fixed in stone, the usual rule of thumb in maritime measurement is to use (imperial) miles for horizontal distances across the water surface and (metric) metres and kilometres for vertical depths. Accordingly, I will follow this convention throughout the book. Some further confusion arises over the issue of miles versus nautical miles (a nautical mile is 1.1508 miles). Sources are often vague on this issue and do not specify nautical miles where this might in fact be the case. Alas, there is no clean and simple solution here. All I can do is to specify nautical miles where these are identified as such.

We are more familiar with the myths and fantasies that cling to the ocean than its natural conditions, reflecting our relative ignorance of its spaces and species.

(Alex Farquharson, Director of the Nottingham (UK) Contemporary Art Gallery [see Farquharson, 2013: 6])

Introduction

Like many of us, my knowledge of the deep ocean[1] came initially from the theatre of the imagination. As a child, I was enthralled by the battles against colossal squid, and other underwater creatures, waged by the mysterious Captain Nemo in Jules Verne's literary classic *Twenty Thousand Leagues under the Sea*. In the late 1950s and early 1960s, I became a devoted viewer of the popular American syndicated television series *Sea Hunt*, whose 155 episodes featured veteran Hollywood actor Lloyd Bridges as scuba diver Mike Nelson. Each week, Nelson performed underwater rescues, thwarted crime and located everything from a sunken freighter to submarines and satellites. In one memorable and prophetic episode, 'The Manganese Story' (aired on 4 October 1958), 'Mike discovers a manganese deposit, but an ambitious young geologist, sharks, and an approaching hurricane threaten to silence him before he can inform the government.'[2] As I will discuss in the next chapter, the search for minerals under the sea did not, in fact, get underway until a decade later, in the late 1960s; even then, manganese mining has only become commercially viable within the last decade.

As a teenager, I affixed a poster of 'the Creature from the Black Lagoon' to my bedroom wall. The creature was presented in the 1954 3-D film of the same name as a lost link between land and sea animals from the Devonian period. The 'Gill-Man', as he was also known, has since become iconic in North American popular culture, even once popping up in an episode of *The Simpsons*, where he emerged from Lake Springfield. More reassuringly, the Beatles sang about a romantic escape to a paradise beneath the sea where one could chill in an 'Octopus's garden in the shade'. Later on, these fictional accounts were supplemented by 'real' snippets of knowledge about the deep gleaned from *National Geographic*, aquarium visits and television documentaries on PBS and the Discovery Channel. These featured oddly shaped marine creatures that looked like nothing ever seen before, brightly hued corals under threat from human incursion, and deep-sea divers in steel cages being battered by bloodthirsty sharks.

Today, the ocean is on the verge of being transformed from a 'half-known life' of 'submarine aliens' (Hoare, 2013: 14–15) to an emerging focus of global attention and concern. In 2008, the United Nations General Assembly decided that, starting in 2009, 8 June would henceforth be designated by the United Nations as 'World Oceans Day'. For World Oceans Day, 2012, the Empire State Building in New York City was lit up in the evening in white, blue and purple, representing the different levels of the ocean. While 'Brangelina' (the celebrity Hollywood couple Brad Pitt and Angelina Jolie) still appear focused on human rights activism, fellow 'A-list' celebrity Leonardo DiCaprio has discovered the plight of the oceans, as well as other environmental causes such as opposition to the Alberta tar sands.[3] A diving enthusiast and environmental activist, in June 2014 DiCaprio announced a $7 million pledge at the State Department's 'Our Oceans' conservation and preservation event to fund organizations and communities that are establishing marine reserves. Decrying 'the Wild West on the high seas', DiCaprio told the gathering, 'We're plundering the ocean and its vital resources, and just because we can't see the devastation from dry land doesn't mean it's any less dangerous' (Stanek, 2014; Warren, 2014).

Perhaps even more telling was a report that same day in the *Washington Post* revealing that US President Barack Obama would seek to ban fishing and energy exploration in a large area of the central Pacific Ocean using his executive powers (see Chapter 4). 'The effects of climate change',

Obama said, 'require new environmental protections' (Snyder, 2014). A month later, the Global Ocean Commission, a high-level initiative captained by 17 blue-chip politicians, heads of major organizations and business leaders, including the former President of Costa Rica (José María Figueres) and former Prime Minister of Canada (Paul Martin), released their final report, *From Decline to Recovery: A Rescue Package for the Global Ocean*. Human activity, the Commission Report says, has put the world's oceans on a dangerous trajectory of decline, threatened right now by climate change, overfishing, plastic pollution, acidification, oil and gas spills; and, in the future, by deep-sea mineral mining, biological prospecting (bio-prospecting) and geo-engineering. In a groundbreaking analysis of data from hundreds of sources, ranging from fossil records to statistics on modern container shipping, fish catches and seabed mining, a team of American scientists concluded that humans are causing unprecedented damage to the oceans. 'We may be sitting on the precipice of a major extinction event,' one of the study's authors ventured (Zimmer, 2015).

While there is a critical mass of scientific knowledge that illuminates and interrogates oceans from the various vantage points of marine biology, oceanography, physical geography, international law, global institutions/governance and environmental sustainability, it is more unusual to find research undertaken explicitly from a social science perspective. Until quite recently, the oceans remained 'outside of history'; it is only in the last decade that the sea was finally recognized as one of the new frontiers for environmental historians (Bolster, 2006; Endfield, 2009). With the exception of the establishment of a research stream on maritime sociology within the European Sociological Association, 'the sea remains generally a stranger to contemporary sociology' (Cocco, 2013: 5). Traditionally, the world's ocean has received much less attention from geographers than has the terrestrial sphere. Most work in the sub-discipline of marine geography has tended to be descriptive, confirming the impression among many non-marine geographers that, in the words of Philip Steinberg (1999: 367), 'the ocean (or the sea, an alternate term) is an uninteresting abyss that separates the places that "matter", a marginal region that has little commonality with or impact on the physical and social processes that characterize the rest of the world.' In addition to Steinberg's own pioneering work, one notable exception to this is Martin Glassner's (1990) book *Neptune's Domain*, commissioned in the wake of the signing of the United Nations Convention on the Law of the Sea (see Chapter 2 of this book).

In the present volume, I examine the past, present and future of deep oceans, employing a perspective informed by a combination of sociological constructivism and critical geopolitics. From this vantage point, the 'deep' is, on the one hand, a physical site sculpted by ocean currents, water temperature and pressure, seeps,[4] seamounts (undersea mountains) and hydrothermal vents and, on the other, a human construct shaped by geographical knowledge, legal definitions, political ambitions and popular cultural texts involving conjecture, fantasy and speculation. One example of this is the distinction between the *deep seabed* portion of the high seas, where mining activity is supervised by the United Nations through the auspices of the International Seabed Authority (ISA), and the *water column* portion, where it is not. Another example is the *Exclusive Economic Zone* (EEZ) (see Chapter 2), which was created by UNCLOS (United Nations Law of the Sea Conference) III on 10 December 1982 and entered into force on 16 November 1994. Extending outward for 200 nautical miles, and beyond in the case of continental shelves, the EEZ is collectively constructed by incorporating geographical, scientific and legal aspects. As for the *continental shelf*, it has recently been transformed from a definition 'rooted' in geo-science, which describes it as the relatively shallow seabed area adjacent to the coast and landward of the continental slope, to a legal-juridical definition that extends and prolongs it to 'encompass the whole continental margin [the area of the sea floor between the coast of a continent and the plains of the deep ocean floor] and not only its inner, shallow parts in the scientific sense' (Brekke, 1997: 39).

Each of these examples incorporates a kind of 'volumetric understanding', whereby the ocean is divided up and classified both vertically and horizontally.[5] As Stuart Elden (2013) points out, we all too often think of the spaces of geography as areas or surfaces, not volumes possessing height and depth.

Thinking of the ocean as a volume rather than an area avoids the trap of treating geopolitics as a flat discourse that privileges claims to territory.

A Discursive Approach to Studying Deep Oceans

The Nature of Discourse

Discourse refers to an interrelated set of storylines which interpret the world around us, and which become deeply embedded in societal institutions, agendas and knowledge claims (Hannigan, 2014: 72). It is enacted through a number of familiar devices of linguistic production: framing, metaphors, narrative and rhetoric. As Tom Mels (2009: 386) suggests, 'the myriad things, processes, and relations we call environment, how they work, and how we should act toward them, are inherently discursive problems.' That is, they are socially constructed and conveyed by language. By extension, environmental issues 'do not present themselves in well-defined boxes labeled radiation, national parks, pandas, coral reefs, rainforest, heavy metal pollution, and the like' (Dryzek, 2005: 8); rather, these are defined and elaborated through discursive interpretations and practices.

Contemporary discussions of discourse inevitably link it to the exercise of power. Invoking the path-breaking work of the French social theorist Michel Foucault (1980), most writers who privilege discourse understand it to be a form of 'soft power'. Put simply, soft power is the ability to get what you want through attraction rather than coercion (Mathiason, 2007: 16; Nye, 2004). As such, it is a way of overriding institutions such as the state and church to control agendas and to incorporate individuals into relations of domination without having to resort to the use of force. Rather than being imposed from the top downwards, however, discourse takes the form of an ongoing cultural contest in which some players possess more resources than others. This is very much the case with environmental discourse, where the ways in which we speak, think about or act upon the biogeophysical world all take place within particular constellations of power (Mels, 2009: 387).

One important form of discourse is what is known as 'policy discourse'. Steinberg (2014: 113) emphasizes that an invaluable source of insight into policy discourse can be the *policy document*. Policy documents may not be the only means by which discursive constructions of place are achieved and reproduced, but they are a useful portal through which to understand how statespersons frame problems and solutions. Vivian Schmidt (2008), a leading constructivist scholar in the discipline of political science, distinguishes between two fundamental forms of policy discourse: *coordinative discourse* among policy actors (civil servants, elected officials, experts, organized interests, activists) and *communicative discourse* between policy actors and the public at large. The former is a closed loop, wherein policy discussion and formation take place in a space isolated and shielded from public consciousness. By contrast, communicative discourse occurs openly in the political policy sphere and involves the deliberation on and legitimation of political ideas and their presentation to the general public. It is not unusual to find that these two forms of policy discourse function more or less separately. For example, state-of-the-art approaches to natural disaster mitigation and prevention that focus on vulnerability, risk reduction and adaptation are normally confined within coordinative as opposed to communicative discourse, resonating weakly in the public sphere, where humanitarian appeals for aid to stricken communities continue to dominate (Hannigan, 2012: 141).

Discourse and Critical Geopolitics

The concept of discourse plays a central role in *critical geopolitics*, a sub-field of political geography that first emerged in the 1990s. Practitioners of critical geopolitics study how government policy, wars and political events are depicted in 'texts' such as maps, speeches, policy documents and popular media (cartoons, comic books, films, newspapers, magazines, photographs) (see Dodds, 2013). Rather than being just representational, however, texts are said to be capable of influencing and in some circumstances even constructing the political world. Thus, the terms 'Iron Curtain', 'Third World' and 'rogue state', commonly utilized by politicians, diplomats, journalists and academics in the 1960s and 1970s, constituted more than geographical metaphors or descriptors. Rather, they generated a simple model of the world that informed foreign and security policy making, while at the same time powerfully shaping how the public at large understood the political geographies of the Cold War (Dodds, 2007: 4–5).

Martin Müller (2013: 54) observes that discourse acts as a 'conceptual linchpin' in critical geopolitics. As such, it possesses power, produces space and is bound up with questions of politics and ideology. Accordingly, Edward Said's seminal work *Orientalism* (1978) can justly be regarded as the first work of critical geopolitics insofar as it shows how the Western world constructed the 'Orient' as exotic and inferior. In a similar key, Frederick Turner's (1893) 'frontier thesis' exerted considerable influence in the late nineteenth and early twentieth centuries on both academic and popular imaginaries of the West and American civil society (see Chapter 1).

Textual deconstruction in critical geopolitics has an uneasy relationship with human agency. On occasion, critical geopolitical analysts seem convinced that texts and discourse actually have *agency*, that is, that they are able to act on their own to challenge knowledge claims, construct (or deconstruct) meaning, produce publics and structure policies and politics. This is especially the case where discourses are bound up with everyday social practices. At other times, critical geopolitical researchers are more cautious, acknowledging only that discourses are socio-cultural resources that enable and constrain people's construct of meaning about their world (Müller, 2013: 57). In any case, discourse can never 'act' in a sociological sense – only people can do that (Hannigan, 2012).

Some of the most advanced work that has been undertaken from this perspective has focused on *critical polar geopolitics*. This interrogates 'the intersections between territories and non-territories, legal regimes, knowledges, resources and public culture that combine to construct and represent the Arctic and Antarctic as spatial entities' (Powell and Dodds, 2014: 9). A recent paper by Jason Dittmer and his co-authors (2011) highlights this treatment. The authors cast Arctic geopolitics as an emergent discourse, which they define as 'a relatively organized assemblage of power/knowledge – via the dynamic assembly and networking of multiple elements across a wide variety of sites' (2011: 1). They say that the standard 'neo-realist' depiction of the Arctic as 'an opening, shifting and potentially chaotic space' doesn't tell the whole story. In this widely circulated, orthodox version, a decrease in polar sea ice cover attributable to global climate change has spurred a host of new opportunities, possibilities and dangers. Dittmer et al. cite a piece by Scott G. Borgerson (2008) in the international relations journal *Foreign Affairs* that describes a new 'scramble for resources' in the region involving the five Arctic Ocean coastal states and their national security interests. This is symbolized by the widely publicized 'planting' of a Russian flag at the bottom of the Arctic Ocean during a 2007 polar expedition. Echoing the nineteenth-century competition by European imperialist powers for geopolitical supremacy in Central Asia, a 'Great Game' is currently said to be taking place at the top of the world among the superpower nations (China, Russia, the United States) with a supporting cast of regional political players (Canada, Denmark, Norway).

Dittmer and his colleagues suggest that 'there is far more to geopolitics in the "High North"' (2011: 11). Spatial orderings of the region have historically been conditioned by a variety of images, fantasies and projections of frontier masculine exploration and adventure. The authors explore these via three examples: a pair of 2009 Arctic exhibitions in London; the 2005 Russian polar expedition; and ongoing 'sovereignty patrols' by the Canadian Rangers, a unit of the armed forces which engages in patrols and surveillance in the Arctic North. This alternative reading nourishes the prevailing discourse of an escalating 'Arctic race' for wealth, resources and sovereignty, but it is more nuanced and historically rooted. The same argument could be made for the importance of a 'masculine' political style. This is illustrated by news clips of Russian President Vladimir Putin skydiving, skiing down a volcano and hugging a polar bear (likely sedated) on a trip to Russia's Arctic North; and by Cossacks on horses whipping Pussy Riot protesters at the Sochi Olympics, both of which help to legitimate Russian national identity politics, as manifested in military incursions into Crimea and eastern Ukraine.

The Discursive Construction of the Ocean

Published in 2001, geographer Philip Steinberg's book *The Social Construction of the Ocean* remains the seminal, and indeed the only, full-length treatment of human–marine interactions that deliberately adopts a discursive perspective. Whereas most studies of marine areas treat the ocean exclusively as a *resource* space used *by* society, Steinberg views it as a *social* space, a space *of* society (2001: 6). He identifies discourse construction as the third pillar of the *territorial political economy perspective* that he employs to analyse the social construction of ocean space in the modern era (the other two pillars being use and regulation). The author offers this as a contrast to, and improvement on, traditional perspectives that treat the ocean exclusively as a resource space designed and managed by land-based societies for commercial and military advantage. In Steinberg's view, the ocean is 'simultaneously an arena wherein social conflicts occur and a space shaped by these conflicts' (2001: 20).

It is rare to find an approach to nature, especially that which puts representation or discourse at the centre, which attempts to fuse radical political economy and social construction. In so doing, Steinberg calls to mind the work of several political ecology scholars (e.g. Stephen Bunker, Paul Cicantell) who wrote in the 1990s about discursive struggles on the socially and geographically remote extractive periphery. Paul Cicantell (1999) published a case study of the Tucurui dam project in the eastern Amazon region in which he demonstrated that a discourse of development promoted by powerful external actors (the Brazilian government, a Japanese private consortium) was crowding out competing discourses of social justice and environmental preservation, as presented by indigenous people. It incorporates the now familiar assumptions about the problematic interrelationship of resource extraction, economic growth and human progress. Steinberg introduces three primary 'discourses' which he says frequently inform the construction of ocean space. The first category, the *discourse of development*, echoes what political ecology researchers have found for land-based resource frontiers such as the Amazonian rainforest. Steinberg notes our past tendency to construct the sea as a kind of 'non-territory' that defies any form of development, but argues that this is still consistent with a development discourse of scientific rationality and space-oriented planning. Second, Steinberg cites a *discourse of geopolitics*. For geopolitical discourse the key spatial unit is the territorially defined state, which interacts with the world's other states (Steinberg, 2001: 34). Geopolitical discourse constructs the sea as external to the territory of political society. As with the discourse of development, it is assumed that the ocean is a void, but, rather than being *developable*, the goal is to make it *governable*.

Steinberg's third category is the *discourse of law*. This considers whether the sea is immune to social control and order. It is presented here as an external space, a 'lawless other'. The prevailing idea in legal discourse is that of mutually exclusive sovereign nation-state territories representing the rule of law and space of society. For example, as the Law of the Sea evolves to permit the extension of the continental shelf, nation states assume legal or at least legally sanctioned economic control over previously unregulated ocean space. All three of these discursive constructions have been significantly buttressed by cartographic representations of ocean space. A map not only represents a pre-formed reality but it also *constitutes* that reality, especially in places like the deep ocean that are likely never to be encountered during the everyday lives of a map's viewers (Steinberg, 2001: 35).

Steinberg locates his territorial political economy within several macro-theories of capitalist spatiality, notably world-systems theory, which was first developed by Immanuel Wallerstein, an American sociologist, in the 1970s. Perhaps reflecting his book's publication date of 2001, he does not substantially address *neoliberalism*, which, as Becky Mansfield

(2004: 313) noted a decade ago, 'is becoming a dominant mode of ocean governance', especially with reference to ocean fisheries.[6] In neoliberal regulation, states and markets act in concert, enclosing the oceans as state property, creating, devolving and enforcing property rights (2004: 315). Despite the title of Steinberg's book, this is more a work of political economy than of social constructivism. In his review of the book in the *American Journal of Sociology*, my environmental sociology colleague Mike Bell (2003: 218) writes: '[A]lthough Steinberg tries to develop a dialectic approach, one side in the debate is still privileged. That side is the material not the ideal, as one might assume for the usual association of the term *constructionism* with discourse and representation.'

In the present volume I share some of Steinberg's key assumptions – notably, that the ocean is both a space of society and an arena of social conflict. However, I am less interested in framing ocean-state constructions within a theoretical framework that focuses primarily on the material organization of society or the global economic order. Rather, as the title indicates, I focus on how the *geopolitics* of the deep has been constructed within the parameters of four competing narratives (see below). Only one of these ('Sovereignty Games') incorporates a standard understanding of geopolitical discourse as 'the representation of space as constructed as a result of nation states interacting with other nation states', a mode of thinking that Steinberg (2001: 34) criticizes for treating the ocean as an empty 'force-field'. Although the book is organized by these storylines, it is not focused exclusively on texts and representations to the exclusion of political economy, a criticism often directed against critical geopolitics by scholars from the 'radical geopolitics' school of thought (Mercille, 2013: 133–4). Indeed, I have made a concerted effort to expose the political economic dynamics of deep-ocean exploration and exploitation, using the method of historical description and analysis rather than critical interrogation. I adopted this approach because I assume most readers only possess scattered knowledge about the deep and would appreciate an informed and readable overview.

The Geopolitics of the Deep: Four Narratives

In this book, I argue that the contemporary geopolitics of the deep ocean is constructed through and around four competing *master narratives* (big stories), which I have labelled: Oceanic Frontiers; Governing the Abyss; Sovereignty Games; and Saving the Ocean. Rather than being completely self-contained and mutually exclusive, these narratives frequently overlap, collude and collide within a 'discursive policy field' (Hannigan, 2012). For example, territorial claims by coastal states to extensions of the continental shelf beyond 200 nautical miles are pursued under the legal auspices of the UN Commission on the Limits of the Continental Shelf (CLCS) (Governing the Abyss narrative); undertaken, at least in part, to secure control over untapped seabed natural resources (oil, gas, minerals) (Oceanic Frontiers narrative); and treated as a geopolitical contest in which political and military strategizing is front and centre (Sovereignty Games narrative).

The four narratives differ substantially in the way they perceive the *oceanic commons*. Commons are collectively managed, shared resources (Milun, 2011: 1). They can range from very small (an apartment complex parking lot) to vast (the high seas, outer space) (Buck, 1998: 5). Garrett Hardin, the American microbiologist and ecologist, made the term iconic in his 1968 essay in *Science*, 'The Tragedy of the Commons'. Hardin drew an analogy between the medieval English village commons, used by locals for livestock grazing, and the contemporary resource commons. *Global commons* are areas of the earth that are not owned by any particular country, and to which all nations have legal access (Aplin et al., 1995: 230). Just as medieval pastures were overexploited and exhausted, without international cooperation, the global commons faces the same fate. A good example of this is overfishing. According to the Brundtland Commission, 'Only the high seas outside of national jurisdiction are truly "commons"; but fish species, pollution, and other effects of economic development do not respect these legal boundaries' (World Commission on Environment and Development, 1987: 262). There appear to be only two alternatives to the tragedy of the commons: divide the resources or depend on explicit institutions and rules to manage it (Bederman, 2008: 71). Oceanic Frontiers is the most laissez-faire of the narratives in its treatment of the commons. The deep is depicted here as a 'resource cornucopia'. All that is required is that it be 'harvested' wisely and properly. The Sovereignty Games narrative does not accept the notion of the commons as constituting common property. Rather, the oceans collectively constitute a chessboard on which political moves are strategically made and territory is claimed. From this vantage point, 'No nation can be a pretender to global influence without a strong maritime presence' (Marx, 1981: 3). The Governing the Abyss narrative embraces the idea of 'sharing the commons' and the 'abyss' refers as much to a physical feature as it does to a sense that these spaces are beyond the regulatory geographies of state sovereignty. This is embodied in the concept of the 'common heritage of [hu]mankind', a guiding principle behind the United Nations Law of the Sea Convention (LOSC), the cornerstone of modern ocean law. To be sure, the tools of global governance are valued here, but first and foremost as a way of redressing the fundamental inequality between have and have-not nations. Saving the Oceans comes closest of the four deep-ocean narratives to subscribing to Hardin's analogy of the 'tragedy of the commons'. It doesn't matter how equally and justly the spoils are divided if, in the end, ocean resources are totally exhausted or the sea floor is contaminated. Consistent with the position each of the four deep-ocean narratives takes towards the maritime commons, I have subtitled each of the chapters that constitute the body of this book as: Harvesting the Commons; Sharing the Commons; Claiming the Commons; and Protecting the Commons.

In the scholarly field of international relations, there have been two dominant paradigms: realism and idealism. The *realist* paradigm assumes that states are the lead actors on the world stage and that power drives all politics. Sovereignty – the idea that states possess exclusive authority over their territory and population – forms the foundation of their rule. By contrast, *idealism* (or liberalism) holds that states compete not only in the international arena among themselves but also with non-state actors such as multinational corporations,

IGOs (intergovernmental organizations), NGOs (non-governmental organizations), global advocacy groups and epistemic communities. The second part of the twentieth century, it is said, was characterized by a move from a world dominated by a single chessboard – the strategic diplomatic one associated with a realistic perspective – to a world dispersed into a variety of chessboards (Rochester, 2006: 24), as might be explained by the idealist paradigm. In recent years, a third paradigm,[7] *constructivism*, has emerged. Constructivists argue that both realism and idealism share an interest-based explanation of international relations, where actors are essentially self-interested and calculating, whether driven by national interests or mutual interests (Rochester, 2006: 30). Constructivists put a premium on the power of the idea. It is not interests that shape international politics any more, they say, but the emergence of new normative beliefs and knowledge. This is typified by the ascendance of humanitarian intervention as a force that shapes the relations in the international community.

As can be inferred from its title, the Sovereignty Games storyline is firmly anchored in the realist paradigm. The contemporary geopolitics of the deep is treated as simply the next chapter in a narrative that goes back to the Cold War – a dominating theme of global geopolitics in the second half of the twentieth century (Sachs, 2006) – when US and Soviet submarines shadowed one another beneath the Arctic and North Atlantic oceans. Today, submarines still circle beneath the North Pole. However, the theatre of action has now shifted as well to the Antarctic, the South China Sea and the Indian Ocean. Furthermore, an expanded roster of nation states beyond just the Cold War superpowers are increasingly chasing sovereignty claims by trying to stretch their territory through claims filed with the United Nations agency tasked with determining the outer limits of continental shelves.

By contrast, the Governing the Abyss narrative is best appreciated using the idealist paradigm. Consistent with the notion of multiple chessboards, the process of establishing and enforcing the Law of the Sea unfolds both in the arena of conventional geopolitics and in a policy field that includes a wide array of non-state actors, most notably a thick roster of IGOs that are part of or affiliated with the United Nations.

Although it reflects a strong commitment to liberal values of humanitarianism and justice, the Governing the Abyss narrative is ultimately interest-based. Specifically, the 'common heritage of [hu]mankind' principle which shaped the Law of the Sea Convention is fundamentally a clarion call for redistributing deep-ocean resources amongst the Global North and South in a more 'equitable' manner. The Oceanic Frontiers narrative combines elements of both realism and idealism. Undeniably, the exploitation of new sources of mineral and biological wealth on the deep seabed, in seamounts and hydrothermal vents is closely articulated with the *realpolitik* of nations. Note, for example, the contemporary 'scramble for resources' in the Arctic, the South Atlantic and the Indian Ocean (Chapter 3). At the same time, the deep ocean constitutes a complex terrain in which the various key players invariably have competing interests and outlooks. For example, Nautilus Minerals, Inc., a leading miner of sulphide deposits and sea-floor polymetallic nodules in the Pacific region, has faced challenges and delays to their Solwara 1 project both from the Papua New Guinea government and from conservationists (see Chapter 1).

Finally, the Saving the Ocean narrative is best explained by turning to the constructivist paradigm. Rather than embracing interest politics, its centre of gravity is an idea: that the deep ocean constitutes a unique and threatened ecology. This being so, ocean scientists and environmental activists are duty-bound to fill knowledge gaps about deep-sea ecosystems and the impacts that human activities are having on them. Thus, HERMES (Hotspot Ecosystems Research on the Margins of the European Seas), a major international research project on Europe's deep seas, describes its brief as to 'provide new insights into the biodiversity, structure, functions and dynamics of ecosystems along Europe's deep-ocean margin . . . with the objective of linking research and policy and providing policymakers and stakeholders with good, relevant and timely scientific knowledge in support of European and international deep-sea governance' (HERMES, 2006).

Scientists have played a key part in determining how we understand and act towards deep oceans. In so doing, the nature of their participation varies widely, and this is reflected in the nature of the roles they play in each of the four narratives discussed in this book. Consistent with the Oceanic Frontiers narrative, many researchers, past and present, have not hesitated to act as partners in the exploration and economic exploitation of the deep oceans. Geological oceanographers, for example, have carried out projects 'in support of implementing and optimizing the exploitation of living resources, and in monitoring oil and gas fields, manganese nodule deposits and other mineral resources' (Vallega, 2001: 7). Others from the scientific world have formed 'epistemic communities' (transnationally organized advocacy networks who offer scientific-technical advice to political decisionmakers) dedicated to protecting ocean biodiversity and health. As I note in Chapter 4, the Saving the Oceans narrative has been embedded in and promoted by several academic 'crisis disciplines', notably ecological economics and biological oceanography. One would think that scientists would instinctively shrink from the geopolitical manoeuvring that characterizes the Sovereignty Games narrative. But, as I show in Chapter 3, there is a long history of collaboration between ocean science and the military, especially during the Cold War, when agencies such as the US Office of Naval Research provided the lion's share of funding to leading oceanographic institutions such as the Woods Hole Oceanographic Institution (WHOI), the Scripps Institution of Oceanography and the Lamont Geological Observatory of Columbia University (see Doel et al., 2006: 607). Today, these close linkages continue to characterize military intelligence activities such as hydrographic surveying and 'cheap stealth', the use of self-powered robotic military systems under the oceans. Finally, academics have long played a central role in constructing and legitimating the Governing the Abyss narrative (Chapter 2). Today, this may be seen in the reliance of nation states on detailed geological and geophysical surveys by scientists and hydrographers as the primary form of evidence in their applications to the UN CLCS to delineate a new continental shelf outer limit. For example, the Institute of Oceanology at the Russian Academy of Sciences has been 'at the forefront of providing the technical expertise so necessary for formal government submissions to the CLCS' (Dodds, 2008: 4). Such legal claims are said to be 'transforming the international politics of underwater prospecting' (Bowcott, 2007), especially in countries such as Papua New Guinea.

Finally, all four narratives of the deep ocean share a conception of the ocean as a previously empty or 'smooth' space that needed to be organized, divided, classified and inscribed (Steinberg, 1999). The Governing the Abyss narrative has taken this the furthest, writing into international maritime law a complicated, and at times bewildering, array of layers and zones, some of which are newly invented. Patches of the deep ocean such as the Arctic have become crowded with legions of geologists and oceanographers engaged in gathering data to support national claims pertaining to the extent of their continental shelves. Mining prospectors, who are exploring the oceanic frontier for copper, manganese, gold and other valuable commodities, also depend on dividing up the deep primarily because they need certainty of title before investing in expensive new technologies and processes. This requires securing exploration and exploitation licences for a demarcated patch of the 'Area' from the International Seabed Authority. National states too are active in inscribing the oceans in a variety of ways: through continental shelf claims; through the activities of their national mining companies; through granting exploration and mining permits to commercial operators within their own EEZs; and through contesting territorial claims, as is increasingly occurring in the South China Sea.

When it comes to deep-ocean space, environmentalists and others who embrace the Saving the Ocean narrative find themselves in a philosophical quandary. On the one hand, they tend to subscribe to a holistic perspective that rejects the imposition of 'artificial' boundaries onto the deep oceans. As Canadian environmental icon David Suzuki says about the dashed hopes for a global climate treaty, 'Copenhagen was trying to deal with something that didn't belong to anybody – the atmosphere – through the lenses of borders, which the air doesn't care about, and the economic interests of 192 countries. We were trying to force nature into our agenda' (Wente, 2012). The same, of course, holds true for the oceans. On the other hand, many marine biologists and environmental activists are passionately committed to 'zoning' as their preferred method of maritime management and to advocating for marine protected areas in places like the Ross Sea. This dictates that large areas of the ocean be protected through demarcating and legally proclaiming dozens of marine reserves and other marine protected areas worldwide. The corollary here is that once designated, these areas need to be patrolled and regulated to keep out intruders such as illegal fishing vessels. Ocean space, then, is rapidly being subdivided into a patchwork quilt of 'striated' space. In their book *A Thousand Plateaus*, the French poststructuralist philosophers Gilles Deleuze and Félix Guattari (1987) conceive of space as produced by the dialectic between striated and smooth space. The former is organized around the notions of territory, regulation and governance, while smooth space is fluid, nomadic and de-territorialized. For Deleuze and Guattari, the sea is intrinsically the archetype of all smooth spaces but over the centuries it has increasingly encountered the demands of strict striation (Milun, 2011: 108). This process took hold in premodern times with the gradual striation imposed by lines of longitude and latitude and has continued in spades with the adoption of international agreements such as the Law of the Sea. Similar to the Disney theme parks, the more the oceans are composed of striated space, the more they become subject to a high degree of control and surveillance. This is a subject to which we shall be returning throughout the book. It is especially evident in the aggressive actions of nation states to legally extend their EEZs outward from the present limits of continental shelves, and in the efforts of conservationists to establish massive patrolled oceanic marine protected areas that are off limits to mining, fishing and other environmentally exploitative activities.

1

Oceanic Frontiers: Harvesting the Commons

In the last decade, media reports of an oceanic 'gold rush' have been appearing with increasing frequency. Recently returned from a trip to the Caribbean on the research vessel RRS *James Cook*, BBC science editor David Shukman filed an online dispatch, 'UK Seabed Resources Joins Deep-Ocean Mineral-Mining Rush'. A subsidiary of the British arm of aerospace giant Lockheed Martin, UK Seabed Resources has announced plans for a major prospecting operation in the Eastern Central Pacific Ocean. 'A new and controversial frontier in mining is opening up', Shukman (2013a) reported, 'as a British firm joins a growing rush to exploit minerals in the depths of the oceans.' In a follow-up piece two months later, Shukman (2013b) opined that 'the prospect of a deep sea "gold rush" opening a controversial new frontier for mining on the ocean floor has moved a step closer.' While remaining worried about the negative environmental costs that might ensue in this new era of deep-seabed mining, Shukman nonetheless situates these events within a widely understood storyline of resource frontiers in distant locations being overrun by a 'rush' of prospectors hoping to find their fortune. This evokes what Richard Slotkin (1992: 18) calls the 'bonanza frontier' model of development.

Shukman is not alone in fearing that this twenty-first-century frontier development may be problematic. Speaking at a 2006 workshop in Brussels convened to discuss the international aspects of deep-sea governance, Kristina Gjerde, policy adviser at the International Union for Conservation of Nature (IUCN), emphasized the irresponsible 'frontier mentality' that deep-sea users are prone to embrace. Some actors, she noted, 'adopt opportunistic strategies, depleting resources in one locale and then moving on to another place' (HERMES, 2006). A year earlier, a writing team at the international marine conservation organization Oceana had expressed a similar sentiment. 'Until recently', they concluded, 'the deep sea remained the final frontier in humanity's incessant search for exploitable resources. Technology has now broken the barriers of depth and distance from shore, to create unsustainable trends in exploitation that are seriously damaging deep-ocean ecosystems' (Roberts et al., 2005: 20).

In fact, similar excitement over an oceanic gold rush had arisen half-a-century earlier. As Maria Gavouneli (2007: 133) tells it, 'The word was at the time that untold riches awaited humankind in the deep black yonder – and the international community cracked at the seams in the effort to contain this new gold rush in the seas.' However, the opening of the oceanic mining frontier was delayed, largely owing to technical challenges, low global market metal prices and the inability of resource companies to raise investment funds in capital markets (Littleboy and Boughen, 2007: 3).

In this chapter, I discuss the powerful discursive notion of the 'oceanic frontier'. The primary narrative thrust here frames the deep as a 'cornucopia', a land of plenty whose fabulous mineral and biological wealth is just waiting to be harvested. Opening this 'final frontier' is presented as the most recent chapter in a history of deep-sea exploration that began a century-and-a-half ago. The deep ocean is valuable not just for its breathtaking array of geological formations and previously unknown fauna and flora, but also for its potential to 'save' humankind by providing unlimited energy, low-cost, high-grade minerals and miracle drugs. Thanks to technological innovations such as deep-sea submersibles and robotic machines, together with increasingly sophisticated scientific methodologies, the commercial potential of the underwater frontier, first imagined in the 1950s, is soon to be realized.

Frontiers and 'Frontierness'

Derek Hall (2013: 53–4) argues that 'frontierness' is an idea as much as it is an objective condition. That is, frontiers – the Amazon, the Steppe, the Pampas, the Arctic, the 'Wild' West – are constructed in evocative ways, primarily by people who live far from them. While Hall uses the concept of the frontier to denote areas at the geographical and political margins where the state has difficulty asserting administrative control (e.g. Pakistan's Federally Administered Tribal Areas), his characterization of the frontier as a socially constructed 'imaginary' applies equally well to the deep-ocean frontier.

Another innovative use of the concept of the frontier is to be found in Adam Dixon and Ashby Monk's (2014) analysis of 'frontier finance' (those pension funds and other large institutional investors located outside of major international financial centres). The frontier metaphor, they note, is geographical in the sense that it signifies a line of demarcation between two areas or the territory at the margins of settled and more developed regions. Following Ladis Kristof's (1959: 271–2) classic distinction, Dixon and Monk warn us that a frontier should not be confused with a boundary. Whereas the latter is inner-oriented, considering the periphery only as it relates to the core, the former is outer-oriented: its main attention is directed towards the outlying areas, which are 'places of experimentation (and even lawlessness) where settled patterns of the center are challenged and manipulated' (Dixon and Monk, 2014: 858). While oceanic frontiers are not settled, especially in their deeper regions, they can be conceptualized as places of danger and innovation.

The trope of the frontier is conventionally associated with the 'opening' and 'closing' of the American West. Robert Hine and John Mack Faragher (2007: 5) identify 'frontier' and 'West' as two key words in the American lexicon that share an intimate historical relation. They point to the California gold rush of 1849 as 'the prelude to the exploitation of the Far West' during the second half of the nineteenth century; it inspired the sudden movement of tens of thousands of migrants across the continent to the Pacific coast. These 'forty-niners' overran native homelands, provoking violence between Indian bands and miners, ranchers and the military.

In 'The Significance of the Frontier in American History' (1893), Frederick Jackson Turner famously declared his 'frontier thesis'. He began with the assumption that large areas in North America had until recently been empty and unknown, with plenty of free land for the taking. The advance of American settlement westward produced a series of successive frontiers. In opening up the frontier, migrants conquered the wilderness, bringing with them progress and prosperity. Turner's central idea is that this historical experience of constantly struggling to master the natural, untamed wilderness on successive frontiers constitutes the single most important causal explanation for the development of American culture, and for the emergence of the United States as a nation state (Hilton and van Minnen, 2004: 5–6).

Richard White (1997: 205) argues that Turner masterfully deployed well-established cultural images of log cabins, wagon trains and frontier farms, constructing a powerful historical narrative. Western settlers were depicted not only as courageous and self-reliant pioneers, but also as creators of a distinctly American outlook – practical, egalitarian, democratic – in marked contrast to the more elitist and effete European outlook that had theretofore shaped American life in the East. It wasn't long before Turner's frontier thesis became 'almost an incantation repeated in thousands of high school and college classrooms and textbooks' (White, 1997: 205). For most of the next century, American environmental history was focused primarily on the history of the American West and the idea of the frontier (Endfield, 2009: 227). As Philip Steinberg (2014: 123) notes, Turner created a popular myth of the 'last frontier' that at one and the same time spoke of a geographical *margin* while addressing a cultural *centrality*. This myth appealed simultaneously to those who advocated protecting the unspoiled nature of the West and those who plotted to exploit its untapped resource potential.

In the century or so since Turner proposed his frontier thesis, there have been many attempts by geographers and historians to recast the meaning of frontiers and frontierness. One of the more helpful of these comes from noted British environmental geographer Michael Redclift. Redclift (2006: 34) argues that it is important to distinguish between the traditional *settlement frontier* as described in Turner's frontier thesis and a more robust, conceptually rewarding, but ultimately threatening, notion of frontiers, as represented by the notion of *global commodity frontiers*. Redclift describes these as lands that are looked upon as 'empty' (despite the presence of indigenous people), whose precious materials and commodities are exploited and exported overseas.

Frontiers of the Sea

Several writers have compared present-day exploitation of the oceans to the frontier made famous by Turner's thesis. In his book *Blue Frontier*, environmental journalist David Helvarg (2006: 10) describes this as 'a process of chaotic and rapacious frontier development similar to what took place in the Wild West'. Rather than forts, mining towns, buffalo hunters and cattle ranchers, today you have giant factory trawlers and draggers, oil and gas drillers and deep-sea miners.

In *America's Ocean Wilderness: A Cultural History of Twentieth-Century Exploration*, Gary Kroll (2008) proposes that in the twentieth-century American imagination the ocean assumed many of the very same characteristics that were typically associated with land-based frontier territories in the nineteenth century. These frontier meanings include a trove of inexhaustible natural resources and mineral riches; a place of peril to avoid; an area to be conserved for industrial capitalism; a fragile ecosystem requiring stewardship and protection; and a seascape of inspiration. It is not surprising, Kroll says, that Americans make reference to the western frontier in order to understand other frontiers like the ocean or outer space, insofar as humans typically make reference to the familiar to help them understand the unknown. Kroll (2008: 1) cites a comment by Sylvia Earle, the prominent author and deep-sea diver, who told listeners in a 2002 address on (US) National Public Radio, 'So little of the ocean has been seen, it is like the early days of exploring the American West.'

In his text *Marine Conservation Biology: The Science of Maintaining the Sea's Biodiversity*, Elliott Norse offers an extended comparison of ocean- and land-based frontier systems. Patterns of marine frontier discovery, expansion and exploitation, Norse claims, are no different from those in terrestrial frontiers. The essence of the latter is a coherent set of legal, economic, socio-psychological and ecological attributes (Norse, 2005: 424–6). Legally, frontiers are areas having open access to resources; larger, less differentiated jurisdictions than non-frontier areas; and few laws that effectively constrain human activities. Economically, frontiers are places where people scramble to exploit natural resources and use these extensively and wastefully rather than intensively and efficiently. Socio-psychologically, frontiers attract persecuted, disenfranchised, impoverished or entrepreneurial people seeking their fortunes; are where people resolve their disputes by unilateral action or force rather than by negotiation; and reward independence, boldness, ruthlessness and unbridled optimism over social restraint, empathy, cooperation, adherence to laws and nuanced weighing of alternatives. Ecologically, in frontier areas humans decrease the diversity and abundance of animal species; increase the abundance of opportunistic or unusable species; and disrupt biogeochemical cycles.

Norse's self-declared 'general theory of frontier systems' works better when applied to marine ecosystems and practices that occur in coastal waters. By contrast, the deep ocean is inaccessible to most of us, rendering problematic the notion of open access to frontier resources. To reach the seabed, you need to own, lease or borrow a submersible vehicle. While considerably cheaper than spacecraft, nonetheless submersibles are expensive to build and run. In 1976, the annual operational costs of operating *Alvin*, the first and longest-running deep-diving submersible, were estimated to be about $1.2 million, including its mother ship and support crew (Heirtzler and Grassle, 1976). More recently, it has been estimated that a deep-ocean scientific expedition can cost up to $30,000 per day with a minimum duration of two weeks (Gavouneli, 2007: 145, n. 10). Clearly, this does not fit the 'bonanza frontier' model of development, which held out 'the possibility of immediate and impressive economic benefits on the basis of low capital outlay' (Powell and Dodds, 2014: 4). While deep-sea miners, bio-prospectors and energy drillers are characteristically bold and entrepreneurial, they should never be confused with the down-on-their-luck settlers, cattle herders, rubber tappers and ore panhandlers of the past who sought their fortunes in the American West, the Yukon or the Amazon. Somewhat rhetorically, Norse (2005: 428) equates the 'hired guns' (lobbyists, litigators) employed by marine user groups to maximize their share and minimize regulation by governments with the hired gunslingers in frontier days who were paid by ranchers to secure land ownership and water rights.

In contrast to land-based frontiers, the creation of the blue frontier 'has failed to spark the public imagination, to inspire grand plans and visions, or even resolve the ongoing competition and struggle over . . . maritime resources' (Helvarg, 2006: 11). One explanation here is that the 'space race' in the 1960s disrupted this possibility. Even today, despite many exciting discoveries such as hydrothermal vents and open-ocean hot spots, the deep sea has 'remained rather remote from public consciousness' (Ramirez-Llodra et al., 2011: 1). Nevertheless, even when stripped of Turner's celebratory 'exulting narrative' (Hilton and van Minnen, 2004: 13), the idea of 'the ocean as a frontier' remains a powerful one, shaping how the deep is presented both in the global media and in international policy circles. Paradoxically, as we are directly exposed to oceans less and less, our fascination seems to grow, as expressed in a wide range of attitudes and behaviours, from aquarium attendance to participation in environmental groups dedicated to ocean stewardship and sustainability (Steinberg, 2008).

David Prescott-Steed (2012) suggests that deep-sea exploration is a frontier science for the twenty-first century. This 'new frontier for visual culture', as he calls it, draws on previously unimagined digital imagery to capture images of giant squids and erupting deep-sea volcanoes, phenomena otherwise unable to be seen by the naked eye. As an object of mass spectatorship, the ocean's abysses remain largely detached from any social or cultural context, framed by a 'documentary' view that is descriptive rather than analytic, and that discourages any critical awareness.

In his reinterpretation of frontier history from an environmental perspective, John Opie (1979: 20, 25) suggests that Americans made the West into a 'dream landscape', perceiving the land (incorrectly, as it happens) as a 'perpetual cornucopia'. Cornucopia means that nature is limitlessly bountiful, with a corresponding unlimited ability to absorb pollutants and adapt to any ecological threat (Dryzek, 2005: 51). The Oceanic Frontiers narrative is cast within this broader cornucopian discourse.

Constructing a Narrative of the 'Oceanic Frontier' at Mid-Century

Marine historian Helen Rozwadowski (2012) dates the emergence of the 'ocean as frontier' metaphor to the period immediately following World War II. This was made possible by a myriad of technological advances, many facilitated by government-sponsored military projects during the war.

This narrative of an underwater frontier, Rozwadowski observes, was assembled by a clutch of 'ocean boosters', primarily scientists, explorers and writers, who dreamed of a new era of development beneath the seas. In their account, fish, plankton and seaweed would be commercially farmed, 'whale ranches' would be established and 'the seafloor would become a construction site, followed thereafter by an industrial zone where workers would participate in undersea oil drilling, submarine cargo shipping, mining and other lucrative endeavors' (Rozwadowski, 2012: 579). In *Frontiers of the Sea: The Story of Oceanographic Exploration* (1960), Robert Cowen, a journalist with the *Christian Science Monitor*, titles his penultimate chapter 'The Promise of Plenty'. Cowen writes,

> The ocean is like a grab bag stuffed with riches out of which man has been taking only those few packages he can lay hands on easily. There are living riches that represent a large and relatively untapped food resource. There are mineral riches spread thinly throughout the water or scattered about the sea bed. One of the promises of oceanography is that an increase

in scientific knowledge of the sea will help man systematically to exploit the resources of the marine grab bag. (Cowen, 1960: 241)

At the forefront of these ocean boosters was the celebrated science fiction writer Arthur C. Clarke, probably best remembered today for his predictions of a moon landing, and for collaborating with director Stanley Kubrick on the script for the iconic motion picture *2001: A Space Odyssey*. Clarke's interest in the ocean paralleled his interest in outer space. A keen scuba diver, salvage agent, underwater photographer and inventor, Clarke used his position as a pre-eminent popularizer of science to promote a vision of the future in which the oceans would become increasingly important in providing food, fresh water, energy and perhaps even a habitable site for undersea living. Clarke was especially fascinated with the possibilities of deep-sea mining. In *The Challenge of the Sea* (1960), he notes the accomplishments of the Dow Chemical Company in extracting bromine directly from the sea on a commercial scale for use in gasoline and photographic materials; and magnesium for use in the aircraft industry. But, Clarke cautions, we must do better in mining the ocean 'if we hope to save our machine-based civilization from collapsing back into the Stone Age through shortage of metals' (Clarke, 1960: 11).

In *Future Shock* (1970), his bestselling look into the world of tomorrow, Alvin Toffler, likewise, foresaw the advent of 'The New Atlantis', wherein the underwater world, immensely rich with oil, gas, minerals, fish and plant life, was poised to become the site of a monumental competitive struggle. This opening of the sea, Toffler predicted, may also bring with it a new frontier spirit – 'a way of life that offers adventure, danger, quick riches or fame to the initial explorers' (Toffler, 1970: 169).

Another celebrated science fiction author of the era, Isaac Asimov, was no less enthused about the potential of the deep ocean for human settlement and exploitation. In August 1964, Asimov paid a visit to the World's Fair at Flushing Meadows and wrote about it in the 'Books' section of the *New York Times*. Asimov was asked to imagine what the World's Fair, as well as our planet itself, might look like

50 years hence in 2014. Population pressure, he predicted, would force increasing settlement of the desert and polar areas.

> More surprising, and in some ways heartening, 2014 will see a good beginning made in the colonization of the continental shelves. Underwater housing will have its attraction to those who like water sports and will undoubtedly encourage the more efficient exploitation of ocean resources, both food and mineral. General Motors shows in its 1964 exhibit the model of an underwater hotel of what might be called mouthwatering luxury. The 2014 World's Fair will have exhibits showing cities in the deep sea with bathyscaphe liners carrying men and supplies across and into the abyss. (Asimov, 1964)

We know now that Asimov was overly optimistic about the prospects of underwater settlement. Nevertheless, it is once again evident how forward-looking thinkers in the 1950s, 1960s and early 1970s thought of the ocean along with deserts, polar regions and outer space as looming frontiers.

Outer Space and Deep Oceans as Frontiers

In December 2004, acclaimed Hollywood filmmaker James Cameron (*Titanic, Avatar, The Abyss*) guest edited a special issue of *Wired* magazine on the 'New Age of Space and Deep Sea Exploration'.[1] In his introductory essay, 'The Drive to Discover', Cameron confesses to *Wired* readers that he made the movie *Titanic* because he was an avid wreck diver and this was the ultimate shipwreck. Thereafter, he was hooked, infected by the deep-sea exploration virus. In March 2012, he went on to set a record by diving 7 miles in a specially designed submarine to the bottom of the Mariana Trench, the lowest point in the Pacific Ocean.

Cameron has been equally fascinated by space exploration. In addition to sitting on the Advisory Council of NASA (National Aeronautics and Space Administration), he has been a financial backer of Planetary Resources Inc., a California start-up company which announced plans in 2012 to mine rare metals from asteroids captured in orbit near the earth (Lewis, 2012). Comparing deep-ocean and space exploration, Cameron writes, 'There are still untold mysteries down there [i.e. in the deep sea] in the dark, enough to fill a hundred years of exploration. Certainly enough to intrigue and compel me for the rest of my life. But of course the only truly infinite frontier is in the other direction' (Cameron, 2004: 190).

Thanks to the iconic television series *Star Trek*, the idea of space as a frontier has become embedded in our popular consciousness since the mid-1960s. In the show's opening narration, William Shatner famously intones, 'Space, the final frontier. These are the voyages of the starship *Enterprise*. Its five-year mission: to explore strange new worlds, to seek out new life and new civilizations, to boldly go where no man has gone before.' Within NASA culture, 'the concept of a frontier – a place of struggle, renewal and destiny – still remains central' (Robinson, 2014: 34). In similar fashion, astropolitical analysts within the Pentagon consider outer space as the last frontier, a place to be conquered, mastered, Americanized and securitized as part of the 'Global War on Terror' (Grondin, 2009: 115). Significantly, perhaps, the US Air Force Command published a journal for space and missile professionals from 2004 to 2011 called *High Frontier*.

Beginning in the late 1950s and early 1960s, 'many of those who were involved in ocean exploration linked the sea to outer space, sometimes pointing to similarities, sometimes to contrasts between these two forbidding, yet promising, environments' (Rozwadowski, 2012: 596). Roger Revelle, esteemed director of the Scripps Institution of Oceanography, begins his introduction to Cowen's *Frontiers of the Sea* by remarking on the 'ironic fact' that there has been a great surge of interest in the ocean and its potential bounty of resources just as we are learning to leave this planet with 'our Sputniks and Explorers, our deep space probes and Project Mercuries' (Revelle, 1960: 9). More often than not, however, the ocean comes out second best in this comparison. In a published report on the possibility of developing a national ocean exploration strategy for the twenty-first century, the (US) National Research Council (2003: 17) remarked, 'This nation and others have invested heavily in the exploration of outer space and the functioning of the human genome and each program has both captured the imagination of the public and produced tangible, valuable discoveries. No similar systematic program exists for ocean exploration, despite its promise.'

Space has been widely perceived as holding the key to answering 'big' scientific and philosophical questions: How old is the universe? How did it form? Is there life beyond our solar system? What are the prospects of colonizing other planets? In his book *Strange New Worlds*, astrophysicist Ray Jayawardhana (2011: 3–4) recalls the first time the concept of another world entered his mind. As a child, he was walking with his father in their garden in Sri Lanka where he grew up: 'He [my father] pointed to the Moon and told me that people had walked on it. I was astonished: the idea that one could walk on something in the sky boggled my mind. Suddenly the bright light in the sky became a place that one could visit.' Later on, the possibility of adventure evolved into pondering the great philosophical implications of other planets being detected.

The deep ocean is vast and mysterious, but it rarely captures our imagination in the same way outer space does. In *Frontiers*, a collection of short essays from the 1980s about new theories and discoveries, Isaac Asimov (1987) devotes two substantial sections of the book ('Frontiers of Space', 'Frontiers of the Universe') to astronomy and the universe, but only three pages to the oceans. Briefly he considers whether hydrothermal vents (chimneys) could be where life first formed on earth, but concludes that temperatures there are too high, causing essential amino acids to break down before forming the proteins and nucleic acids that are essential to life. 'Chronos', a contributor to the online message board 'The Straight Dope', observes that we've already been to the bottom of the Mariana Trench, the deepest part of the ocean. While it's still worthwhile to explore further, its geographical boundaries are finite. By contrast, consider the vast possibilities of space exploration,

> Humans have only been to one other world. Our probes haven't even been to all the planets of our Solar System, much less the moons, comets, asteroids, and other interesting

subjects. Our most distant robotic explorers are less than a hundred times more distant than the Earth is from the Sun, but the closest stars are hundreds of thousands of times more distant. We've still got plenty of frontiers, in space.[2]

Citing the life and writing of Arthur C. Clarke, Rozwadowski (2012) makes a similar point. What makes space a better frontier, she argues, is its infinity. While ocean exploration is destined to end one day, the space frontier is immune to the restrictions of earthly frontiers. That is, while the ocean appears to have seemingly unlimited economic potential, space is 'ultimately judged to be a better frontier because of its potential to serve human spiritual and cultural needs endlessly into the future' (Rozwadowski, 2012: 596). Dreams of leaving earth to colonize other planets resonate more strongly than expectations of fabulous wealth to be derived from the ocean's depths. Whereas outer space is beyond the reaches of earth, we share the planet with the deep ocean; it is 'both a here and an elsewhere' (Farquharson, 2013: 6).

Space exploration assumed a greater urgency during the Cold War than did its marine equivalent. Nonetheless, there was a large body of research on underwater environments leading to better understandings of the seabed, sea ice and acoustics. As will be discussed in Chapter 3, much of this was linked to submarine warfare. When the Soviet Union launched the first artificial, earth-orbiting satellite, *Sputnik*, in October 1957, it shocked America, highlighting the potential for launching intercontinental ballistic missiles from space and using satellites for spying (Hamblin, 2005: 62, 91). In the 1960s, being the first to set foot on the moon became a central policy tenet of the Kennedy administration – at the heart of the 'New Frontier', a political discourse that alluded to the pioneer adventurers of the old 'Wild West' while asserting the importance of closing the 'space gap' between the United States and the USSR (Griffin, 2009: 63).

Beginning in the 1990s, ocean exploration and space exploration started to engage more closely with one another. That's not to say that they had previously operated as two solitudes. As a spinoff from the Apollo space programme, interest in the potential of using space-borne instruments for studying the sea had grown, culminating in the 1964 symposium 'Oceanography from Space', which attracted 150 oceanographers (Guymer et al., 2001: 193). Nonetheless, the two areas really didn't begin a serious conversation until several decades later. Most recently, one shared interest is the survival of extreme life forms in harsh and remote environments. Space scientists have become intrigued with the deep-ocean thermal vents that host newly discovered organisms that exist at temperatures and pressures previously thought to be too high to sustain life (Day, 2008). Similarly, there has been considerable interest in microbes that live without heat or sunlight in water trapped under crusts of ice in the Arctic and Antarctic. If life finds a way to adapt to strange conditions here, scientists ask, why could it not live on Jupiter's moon Europa or Saturn's moon Enceladus, both of which have water trapped under crusts of ice? (Borenstein, 2012).

Another shared issue relates to the legalities of resource exploitation on the frontiers of the deep ocean and outer space, something that was central both to the UNCLOS III negotiations (1973–92) and the Moon Treaty (1979). Over half-a-century ago, Robert Cowen interviewed John Mero, a mineral engineer who wrote a commissioned report for the Scripps Institution of Oceanography on the technical and economic prospects for dredging up manganese nodules from the ocean floor. Mero pointed out that 'there is a legal problem here to match that raised by the exploration of space' (Cowen, 1960: 268). He thought it might make sense to call an international conference to lay down the ground rules before any large-scale open-sea mining was to be attempted.

Deep-Ocean Exploration and Discovery

The idea of the deep ocean as a frontier has long been fuelled and legitimated by an overlapping narrative of exploration (seeking) and discovery (finding). Ever since 1492 when Christopher Columbus sailed off the edge of the known world in search of new trade routes to the Indies, an intrepid band of ship captains, marine scientists, divers, hydraulic engineers, deep-sea miners and drillers have traversed the high seas and descended into the 'abyss' to reveal the wonders of an alien water world.

Typical of this discursive outlook is a book-length pictorial essay 'Secrets of the Sea' compiled by Carl Proujan, a prolific American science writer, editor and filmmaker. Proujan first published 'Secrets of the Sea' in 1971 as Part 3 of *Earth's Last Frontiers*.[3] Nearly two decades later (1990) it resurfaced as Volume 14 of *The Marshall Cavendish Illustrated Encyclopedia of Discovery and Exploration*. Proujan offered readers a whistle-stop tour of ocean exploration, from the deep-sea dredging missions of the early nineteenth century to the manned and unmanned exploration of the deep in submersible vehicles in the 1960s. 'In an age when man has climbed to the peaks of the loftiest mountains, and crossed the frozen wastes of the poles,' he proclaims, 'the depths of the sea remain unconquered. They form the last great frontier on earth' (Proujan, 1973: 331).

Benedict Allen (2002) expresses a parallel view in *The Faber Book of Exploration*, his 800-page 'Anthology of Worlds Revealed by Explorers through the Ages'. Allen doesn't introduce deep oceans until the postscript, which he titles 'New Frontiers: Outer Space, Inner Mind, Underwater, Underground'. He suggests that these 'new frontiers' have been neglected because we previously lacked either the technology or intellectual framework to tackle them. Unlike the interior of Africa crossed by Stanley in the nineteenth century with gun tucked under arm, the plains and fissures of the deep sea are being explored 'by scientists in front of computer monitors using remote imaging' (Allen, 2002: 767). But, unlike Proujan, Allen refuses to call this 'the last great frontier of exploration', on the grounds that the frontiers of knowledge are infinite.

Robert G. Albion (1965: 2) observes that there have long been two prime motives for exploration, frequently occurring in tandem: the hope for national or individual profit and the gratification of geographical and scientific curiosity. European exploration on the African continent in the Victorian age is a prime illustration of this. Intrepid adventurers – Richard Burton, James Grant, John Speke, Henry Morton Stanley, David Livingstone – were dispatched by the Royal Geographical Society to the 'Dark Continent' to solve geographical puzzles that had fascinated Europeans for centuries, most notably locating the source of the Nile. Their exploits were conveyed widely (and sensationally) in the popular press and on the lecture circuit. Underlying much of this excitement was the hope that Africa would provide a source of raw materials to feed the Industrial Revolution, as well as liberating a king's ransom in diamonds, gold and other precious metals (Hochschild, 1999: 27). Drawing on an essay by the novelist Joseph Conrad (1926) on three defining epochs[4] in the history of geographical knowledge, Felix Driver (2001) identifies the nineteenth century as the second of these, the epoch of 'Geography Militant'. By this he means a quest for empirical knowledge about the geography of the earth distinguished by cultures of exploration and empire.

In similar fashion, geographical and scientific inquiry has long been intertwined with commercial motives in the exploration of the seven seas. In the fifteenth and sixteenth centuries, the 'Age of Discovery', John Cabot, Vasco da Gama, Christopher Columbus, Ferdinand Magellan and other seafaring Italian, Portuguese and Spanish navigators sailed off into uncharted waters on the edge of the known world. Initially, this had little to do with probing the secrets of the oceans; they were more concerned with finding new trade routes and territories (Loftas, 1972: 15). David Arnold (1983: 7) points out that five centuries ago Europeans did not contrast the affluent 'North' with the impoverished 'South', as is the case today. Rather, they associated Asia and Africa with their products – gold, jewels, silks, tapestries and spices – and it was the image of these riches that inspired the European seafaring voyages of discovery.

By the eighteenth century, serious scientific maritime observation had begun to take on a new importance. Sir Joseph Banks, an amateur scientist and later head of the Royal Society, helped promote Captain James Cook's three notable trips in the Pacific Ocean between 1766 and 1779, as well as systematic observation of Arctic geography and natural history by several whaling captains. Captain Cook, Rozwadowski (2005: 20, 46) tells us, initiated a new scientific style of exploration that emphasized systematic inventory of natural resources in addition to traditional geographical goals, demonstrating 'prowess, commercial muscle, and cultural superiority'. In the next century, between 1831 and 1836, in another famous voyage of scientific discovery, Charles Darwin sailed around South America on the HMS *Beagle*.

The Challenger *Expedition*

Deep-sea exploration is said to have seriously begun with the HMS *Challenger* expedition (1872–6). Sponsored by the Treasury Museum and the Royal Society of London, and funded by the British Admiralty, the expedition was novel mainly owing to its massive scale (Rozwadowski, 2005: 168). Much of the technology was adapted from items already in use (Deacon and Summerhayes, 2001: 21, n. 1): for example, the underwater dredging technology it utilized had been tried and tested previously on shorter voyages by HMS *Lightning* (1868) and HMS *Porcupine* (1869–70).

Challenger set off with two specific mandates in mind, one commercial, one scientific. The first transatlantic cable had been laid in 1858, but it snapped two years later. The *Challenger* expedition was tasked with identifying obstacles that might impede the future laying and retrieving of telegraph cables in the deep: extreme temperatures; irregularities on the seabed terrain; marine creatures that might attack the cable covers.[5] The ship's 250-member crew included seven scientific researchers – zoologists, botanists, chemists – and even an on-board photographer, under the direction of the well-known Scottish naturalist Charles Wyville Thomson, professor of natural philosophy at the University of Edinburgh. They were especially keen to settle the question of whether the deep oceans hosted fauna of great size and antiquity, members of lost races of living fossils inhabiting a distant and isolated location. These 'evolutionary throwbacks' (Broad, 1997: 35) were suggested by Charles Darwin's *The Origin of Species*, which had been published 13 years earlier.

Over three and a half years at sea and nearly 70,000 miles travelled, a huge amount of data was gathered on temperatures, currents, depths, contours and marine biology, laying the foundation for the science of oceanography (Albion, 1965: 4). The topography of the seabed was charted for the first time, including long, winding mountain ranges that rose all the way to the surface. Thousands of previously unknown species of living creatures were discovered in conditions that had long been considered inhospitable, although none turned out to be living fossils. Brown or black potato-shaped particles hauled up from the seabed turned out to be manganese nodules. In the 1870s, these were little more than scientific curiosities, but today manganese nodules promise to become a leading commodity in deep-sea mining. Indeed, this was anticipated in the *Sea Hunt* episode discussed in the Introduction to this book.

Challenger made a triumphant return to England on 21 May 1876. Thomson was knighted, awarded the Gold Medal of the Royal Society and appointed Director of the *Challenger* Expedition Commission, the purpose of which was to oversee the distribution and detailed study and publication of findings of the vast collection of marine creatures dredged up from the depths of the world's oceans (Guberlet, 1964: 51). The resulting *Report on the Scientific Results of the Voyage of the HMS Challenger during the Years 1872–76* ran to 50 volumes, making it unique in its own century and the largest single natural research project in history prior to World War II (Burstyn, 2001: 51).

The *Challenger* exploration of the depths of the Western Pacific was the oceanographic equivalent of landing on the moon, circumscribing imagination and eroding the mystery of our planet (Hoare, 2013: 17). More than any other single event, the voyage of the *Challenger* and the compilation of its report paved the way for the growth of oceanography as an independent science in the twentieth century (Deacon and Summerhayes, 2001: 21). Additionally, Harold Burstyn (2001: 53) argues that the expedition and report are especially notable as precursors and beacons that pointed the way to the new age of 'big science', characterized by the building of large multidisciplinary teams or coalitions of scientists, politicians, bureaucrats and industrialists.

Frontiers of Ocean Science

In science and medicine, exploration is considered an early component of the research process, the collection of basic observations that guide further, more systematic and controlled study (National Research Council, 2003: 17). This occurs in the laboratory (e.g. identifying a genetic sequence) or in the field (e.g. finding a tropical plant that yields a cure for malaria or cancer), often at what is widely known as the 'frontiers of science'. Exploration constitutes both an activity and a symbol for the process of science itself, where researchers discover new lands through exploring nature's laws (Robinson, 2014: 23).

There were two truly outstanding discoveries in ocean science in the twentieth century. The first was the discovery of mid-ocean ridges and sea-floor spreading, and the synthesis of these findings into a revolutionary theory in earth science known as *plate tectonics* (Prager, 2000: 142). The theory of plate tectonics states that the surface of the earth is made up of a series of flat pieces or plates that are constantly moving. When these plates shift, they are thrust under one another, sometimes colliding and generating deep earthquakes. This is especially evident in the middle of the Atlantic Ocean, where earthquakes and the eruption of lava from the earth's mantle carry the North American plate away from the European plate, forming a new sea floor in the process (Ellis, 1996: 32).

Plate tectonics explains why the continents look like they could fit together like the pieces of a giant jigsaw puzzle. Over 100 million years ago, the continents had been fused together in a much larger supercontinent, but then drifted apart, creating large ocean basins in between. The German meteorologist Alfred Wegener first proposed this 'continental drift' theory in the 1920s, but it was not fully accepted for a very long time, in large part because it wasn't known what force could possibly be strong enough to drive the movement (drift) of entire continents. (Wegener thought, incorrectly, that convection currents might be the answer.) The theory of plate tectonics developed incrementally. However, it was not fully legitimated until the 1960s, when Canadian geophysicist J. Tuzo Wilson contributed several key insights involving hot spots and transform faults (junctions where giant lithospheric plates interact), and geologists Jason Morgan and Xavier Le Pichon accurately determined the number of major plates and how they related to one another.

Deep-sea exploration provided key empirical evidence to validate this theory of moving continents and geological plates, sometimes serendipitously rather than by design. During a period of intense oceanographic research in the 1920s, the German dredge ship *Meteor* carried out one of the first systematic surveys of the ocean floor using an echo sounder, as well as making detailed studies of the temperature and chemical composition of seawater. Given its humiliation by France and Britain after World War I, Germany was anxious to show the world that its ocean science was alive and well. Additionally, there were fervent hopes that valuable seabed minerals might be dredged up, thus helping to pay off Germany's crushing reparations to the Allies. Nearly a century later, the *Meteor* expedition is remembered primarily for its discovery that the Mid-Atlantic Ridge extended around the Cape of Good Hope towards the Indian Ocean in the shape of a rugged mountain range, thereby contributing a key piece to the puzzle of how continental drift occurred.

Fast forward to the late 1960s. With funding from the National Science Foundation, the Scripps Institution of Oceanography and its scientific partners (Lamont-Doherty, Woods Hole, University of Washington, University of Miami) carried out a Deep Sea Drilling Project (DSDP) in the Gulf of Mexico, South Atlantic, Pacific and Indian Oceans as well as the Mediterranean and Red Seas. Operations were carried out from the 10,000-ton drilling ship *Glomar Challenger* (named after the original *Challenger* and Global Marine, the company that owned the ship). Samples collected off Antarctica stirred much interest in the resource potential of the region. Core samples drilled along an oceanic ridge between South America and Africa provided definitive proof for continental drift and seafloor renewal at rift zones. Furthermore, scientific analysis of these samples concluded that the ocean floor is relatively young: no older than 200 million years, as compared to 4.5 billion years for the earth. This strongly suggests that as the sea floor spreads from the rifts, it descends again beneath tectonic plates or is pushed upward to form mountain ranges (IODP, 2007). Kenneth Hsü, a well-known sedimentologist who was aboard the *Glomar Challenger* for this drilling campaign, and later wrote about it in two books (Hsü, 1983, 1992), marvelled, 'The drilling campaign of Leg 3 was one of the greatest triumphs in geology. The theory of sea-floor spreading is right. The unbelievable assumption of a linear rate of sea-floor spreading is correct, at least for the last 70 million years' (cited in Ellis, 1996: 49).

At about the same time, the International Decade of Ocean Exploration (IDOE) (1971–80) was established, largely at the initiative of the marine community in the United States. In keeping with a long history of maritime exploration and discovery, the IDOE was motivated both by the anticipated exploitation of marine resources (agriculture, seabed oil, gas and minerals) and by scientific curiosity (National Research Council, 2003: 21). While the IDOE generally failed to gain much traction, largely owing to underfunding, two international programmes created through bilateral agreements stood out: the 1975 French–American Mid-Ocean Undersea Study (FAMOUS) and POLYMODE, the 1973–81 US–USSR follow-on to the Mid-Ocean Dynamics Experiment (National Research Council, 2003: 23).[6] The former turned out to be especially important. Designed as a comprehensive investigation of a 'typical' section of a mid-ocean ridge near the Azores to determine the nature of the geological processes there, it provided the first observed snapshot of the role played by these ridges in the new global theory of plate tectonics (Oreskes, 2003: 720–1).

The second great discovery is that of hydrothermal vents and seeps, made on the Mid-Ocean Ridge east of the Galapagos Islands in the late 1970s. Robert Embley (2007: 26) describes its significance as follows:

The 1977 discovery of hydrothermal vents on the Galapagos Ridge was one of the most important discoveries of twentieth-century science. It altered our view of life on earth and opened up new possibilities for the very origin of life. An entire new ecosystem was discovered which is based not on photosynthesis, where the food chain is based on solar energy, but on chemosynthesis, where the food chain is based on chemical energy.

From a visual perspective, the most spectacular type of hydrothermal vent system is the 'black smoker'[7] that can be found at most active vent sites. These are chimney-like structures composed of sulphide and sulphate minerals that cap sea-floor vent sites. The 'black smoke' that spews out from them is formed when extremely hot hydrothermal fluid from the earth's interior rapidly exits the chimney opening and mixes with cold seawater, forming a dark particulate (Tivey, 1991/2: 68). This is reminiscent, perhaps, of traditional images of nineteenth-century industrialization. Minerals are both deposited at the vent site and dispersed into the water column.

As Embley hints in the passage quoted above, the discovery of hydrothermal vents sparked a fierce debate in the leading scientific journals over nothing less than the origins of life itself. Of particular scientific importance were certain immobile tubeworms nourished by bacteria in their gut, which they absorbed from the water through branchials (plumes). Some researchers, notably, Jack Corliss (Corliss et al., 1979), who was one of the discoverers of the Galapagos rift animals, proclaimed that this opened up a new frontier in the question of how life began. However, critics such as Stanley Miller and Joseph Bata (1988) disagreed, arguing that Corliss's theory failed each of the three key steps necessary for the origin of life (Ellis, 1996: 124–5), namely: the synthesis of amino acids and other essential organic compounds from the dissolved methane and other gases, initially at high temperatures; the synthesis of peptides and nucleotides by thermal dehydration and other high-temperature reactions; and the synthesis of protocells or RNA-like molecules at some stage in the thermal gradient, and the conversion of these protolife forms into living organisms as the hydrothermal waters emerge from the vents.

Deep-Sea Exploration and Popular Culture

In popular culture, exploration denotes expeditions to exotic, remote corners of the globe: jungles, polar extremities, distant galaxies and the depths of the ocean. Explorers are imagined to be rugged individualists in safari suits or wetsuits, reminiscent of Indiana Jones, the fictional cinematic archaeologist and adventurer. One reason for the emphasis in popular literature on exploration on the ordeals and triumphs of the lone heroic explorer is that most information about journeys to distant lands came from the first-hand accounts of those who made them (Kennedy, 2014: 3). In the realm of deep-sea exploration, Jacques Cousteau (who died in 1997) best fits this profile. Cousteau was a former French Navy commando who became the quintessential diver and lone explorer of the ocean. Bill McKibben (2007a: ix), himself widely recognized as an environmental activist and writer, sums this up, 'For those of us who came of age in the 1960s or '70s, the picture of Jacques Cousteau is fixed forever in our minds. . . . He was as commanding a media persona as Walt Disney (who had his own fantastical world); there were very few foreigners that Americans viewed with more complete trust and admiration' (McKibben, 2007a: ix). Cousteau's maritime exploits are celebrated for all time in American folk singer John Denver's inspiring anthem about the *Calypso*, a former Royal Navy minesweeper that served as Cousteau's research ship for four decades until it sank in a freak accident in 1996. Cousteau's career took off as a result of support from the National Geographic Society Committee for Research and Exploration. His public image soared with the success in the 1950s of his best-selling book and then (with co-director Louis Malle) award-winning film *The Silent World* (1953 and 1956, respectively); and again a decade later with the popular ABC television documentary series *The Undersea World of Jacques Cousteau* (1968–76), produced by David Wolper.

Cousteau was uniquely successful in blending the roles of deep-sea diver and inventor, ocean explorer and concerned conservationist. His signature technical achievement came early on with the co-invention of the patented 'Aqualung', a pressurized, self-contained underwater breathing apparatus (SCUBA) that permitted humans to swim underwater at depths previously considered impossible. Cousteau's discovery of a 2,000-year-old Greek merchant ship led the then-director of the Scripps Institution of Oceanography to call him 'the founder of undersea archeology' (Schiefelbein, 2007: 14).

Cousteau both embraced and resisted the prospect of an oceanic frontier that would be a salvation for humanity. In 1974, he wrote an Introduction ('Manna from the Sea?') to a coffee-table book entitled *The Ocean World of Jacques Cousteau: Riches of the Sea*. The volume was a menu of future possibilities offered by the deep ocean. Solar energy cells that could carry the sun to the bottom of the sea allowing photosynthesis would pave the way for a revolution in mariculture (farming the sea). Mining industrial quantities of 'manganese cobblestones' at long last seemed to be within commercial grasp. Prospecting for 'black gold' (oil) offered exciting commercial possibilities. The deep ocean possessed great potential as a 'marine medicine chest' from which new drugs with exciting possibilities could be produced. In his introduction, Cousteau (1974: 8) warns that when explorers 'open the gates of the ocean or of outer space', we need to exercise caution so as not to duplicate the 'shameless rape of the sea' inflicted in the past by overfishing, the destruction of coral reefs and offshore oil drilling. This environmental message had previously been all but invisible in the boosterist discourse of the 1950s and 1960s. Nevertheless, the overriding message of the book was quite clear: 'The sea is the last unexplored frontier remaining on earth. It offers an unsurpassed adventure to those of us still willing to explore' (Cousteau, 1974: 128).

Gary Kroll detects this same duality in Cousteau's perspective on the deep. On the one hand, he embraced a technologically savvy culture to mediate humans and the ocean: 'More than providing a window to undersea life, Cousteau's books, articles, films and television series highlight an ocean populated by scuba-equipped man-fish, underwater scooters, underwater flying saucers, and housing units. Cousteau created an ocean that was easily explored and imminently habitable through the genius of science and technology' (Kroll, 2008: 7). By the 1970s, however, Cousteau the explorer had turned into Cousteau the environmentalist. Nevertheless, 'he continued to look to the scientific and technological advances that would ameliorate the ocean's environmental problems' (Kroll, 2008: 7).

Today, deep-sea exploration and popular culture are engaging in previously unimagined ways. David Prescott-Steed (2012) argues that digital technology is mediating a new era in deep-sea awareness by making visible what few people otherwise could ever hope to experience, notably the abyssal (sea floor) terrain and hydrothermal vents. In this, we are completely dependent upon scientists and digital media industries to capture the imagery and package it for a range of educational and entertainment purposes. It is telling, Prescott-Steed says, that three-quarters of the deep-sea documentary films ever made have been produced since 2000, many of which are custom-made for IMAX. With increasing rapidity, the textual nature of Western inventions of the deep sea is giving way to visual depictions such as giant squid and 'black smokers' that are better suited to our 'ocular-centric society'.

Underwater Prospecting

Reminiscent of Jules Verne's classic science fiction published in 1870, these modern day explorers are pushing the boundary by taking advantage of tremendous technological advances made in recent decades.

(Nautilus Minerals, 2013: 18)

In the resource sector, exploration has a different meaning than it does in science or popular culture. For energy and mining companies, exploration means locating, drilling, sampling and mapping energy and mineral deposits. Today's exploration and development teams are a far cry from the grizzled 'prospectors' and shady stock promoters who once populated the mining industry. In 1960, Arthur C. Clarke (1960: 121) presciently observed that while 'the great gold rushes of a century ago may be repeated on the sea bed . . . prospectors will not be grizzled old-timers working alone. They will be multimillion-dollar corporations employing armies of scientists and technicians.'

Note, for example, the changing culture of the Prospectors and Developers Association of Canada (PDAC), whose convention is a premier annual event in the mining industry held annually in Toronto. On 9 March 1987, PDAC delegates were shocked by the news that Guy Lamarche, a hustler and night club owner from Northern Ontario, had shot and killed mining stock promoter Timmy Bissonette with a silver-plated pearl-handled revolver on the up-escalator of the Royal York Hotel (Gill, 2012). A quarter-century later, PDAC is now dominated by geologists and analysts, whose interests are more likely to run to such topics as access to capital, mineral exploration tax credits and corporate social responsibility. Rather than talking about staking a claim, conversation on the convention floor today is more likely to run to the CAPEX (capital expenditure) required to work a potential site. In this new, corporatized, mining industry, attention is increasingly focusing on what Maurice Tivey, a senior scientist at the Woods Hole Oceanographic Institution (WHOI), calls a 'new frontier of deep-sea exploration and mining' (AAAS, 2009). The focus here is on the verification and exploitation of previously identified resources in the EEZ of island nations of the southern and western Pacific, notably New Zealand, Papua New Guinea, Tonga and Fiji (Littleboy and Boughen, 2007: 3).

Commercial interest in the deep ocean began in earnest in the late 1960s, thanks in part to a series of technological breakthroughs and geological discoveries. On the initial leg of its 30-month journey in 1968, the *Glomar Challenger* (see above) extracted core samples that revealed the existence of salt domes, an indicator of oil potential. Later on, the crew located traces of oil and gas under 12,000 feet of water and 5,000 feet of sub-bottom material, the first time that oil had been found in a deep-sea area (Cousteau, 1974: 37).

Throughout the early 1980s, oceanographers located several 'hot spots' for polymetallic sulphide deposits. In the autumn of 1981, NOAA (National Oceanic and Atmospheric Administration) scientists under Alexander Malahoff found a massive sulphide deposit on the Galapagos Rift, 500 miles off the Peruvian coast, containing an estimated $2 billion in copper. A year later, Dr Peter Rona of NOAA, leading a team of scientists from the WHOI, discovered a 2-mile-long deposit of manganese and iron along the wall of an underground mountain range on the bottom of the Atlantic Ocean 1,800 miles east of Miami (Simon, 1984: 131).

Currently, there are three forms of deep-sea mineral resources that are being considered for commercial exploitation (Herzig, 2013; Ramirez-Llodra et al., 2011): cobalt-rich ferromanganese crusts covering large seamounts in the

Western and Central Pacific Ocean; manganese and other metal-bearing nodules located on the abyssal plains at depths of up to 5 kilometres, especially in the Clarion–Clipperton Zone (CCZ);[8] and sulphide deposits of copper, lead, manganese, silver and zinc located at the sites of hydrothermal vents along mid-ocean ridges at water depths of 800–2,500 metres. Cobalt-bearing manganese crusts have been known for almost as long as manganese nodules, although the quantities of metals tend to be much higher in the former (Cronan, 1990: 111). Crust mining is the furthest away of the three forms of deep-sea mineral resources from active production; as it now stands, there is currently no useable technology known that can easily break the cobalt crusts off the seamounts. Even so, there has been considerable interest in the crusts for more than three decades. In Japan, prompted by that nation's discovery that cobalt crust deposits lay within 200 miles of the country's coast, in 1985 Prime Minister Nakasone established a committee with representatives of industry, government and academia in order to recommend what future national policy in this field should be (Gibbons and Spagni, 1986: 135). Nearly three decades later (2013), applications for the exploration of cobalt crusts were submitted to the International Seabed Authority by Japan Oil, Gas and Metals National Corporation (JOGMEC), as well as by China Ocean Mineral Resources Research and Development Association (COMRA) and the government of the Russian Federation (International Seabed Authority, 2013).

Sulphides in the sea floor and along ocean ridges constitute considerably larger deposits than do the seabed nodules – some sulphides can weigh as much as 100 million tons. They also grow much faster than do seabed nodules.[9] These mineral residues form near hydrothermal vents where superheated – as much as 404°C – mineral-rich water gushes up through the ocean floor. There are currently 400 known hydrothermal sites, 200 of which are said to be active.

Recovering manganese-rich, polymetallic nodules from the sea floor has been the focus of much of the debate over deep-sea mining. Exploration began at the start of the 1980s and a legal framework and mechanisms for regulation were established at UNCLOS III (see Chapter 2). The first working project of this type, 'Solwara 1', has yet to begin commercial production (see Box 1.1); however, the most recent estimates suggest that mining could start by 2019. The entire emerging deep-ocean mining industry is anxiously awaiting the outcome. Chris Yeats (2012), an ore deposit geologist and team leader at Australia's Commonwealth Scientific and Industrial Organization (CSIRO), observes, 'As Nautilus develops Solwara 1, the mineral industry will be watching closely. Success for Nautilus will signal that marine mining, currently a small niche on global mineral exploration, has the potential to be a major global industry, with the Western Pacific at the forefront.'

Finally, there are a number of other mineral resources whose commercial potential is considerable but about which relatively little is known, or which do not cluster in sufficient quantities so as to make it worthwhile extracting them. Of these, the most important are methane hydrates (see Box 1.2).

Conclusion

More than three decades ago, Geoffrey Kemp, a security and international affairs specialist who once served as a special assistant at the White House, proposed that the exploitation of new resource frontiers has a major impact upon the geopolitical perspectives of states and, therefore, changes the shape of international relations (Kemp, 1981). The quest for new frontiers at a particular point in history, he observes, can be linked to two different sets of explanations. The first, 'micro', explanation incorporates 'ideology and adventure, greed and price, luck and foresight, national interest and anarchy' (Kemp, 1981: 116). For example, maritime exploration in the 'Age of Discovery' (see above) would be interpreted as 'the outgrowth of the renaissance spirit'. The second, 'macro', explanation refers to the interaction of three basic variables: population dynamics, technology and the demand for and supply of scarce resources. Thus, the discovery of the New World may be interpreted as the inevitable result of growing population and rising demand in Europe coupled with the development of new maritime technologies. Both sets of explanations, Kemp says, need to be understood to

Box 1.1 Solwara 1

Solwara 1, a pilot project operated by Nautilus Minerals Inc., may unlock the gates to the deep-sea mining gold rush. A Canadian company headquartered in Australia, Nautilus holds a significant number of exploration licences and applications in various regions in the Pacific Ocean, both for mining polymetallic nodules and for testing the possibility of mining sea-floor massive sulphide deposits in the Exclusive Economic Zone. It has been actively pursuing the commercial exploration and development of mineral resources on the ocean floor, most notably the Solwara 1 deposit, situated in territorial waters off the coast of New Guinea at a water depth of approximately 1.6 km. The company plans to use a fleet of 200-ton, robotic machines,[10] steered from a ship at the surface, to collect the deposits off the ocean floor, then deliver the material to a large, attached surface vessel where the excess water will be removed prior to shipping the remainder directly to smelters in China (Nautilus Minerals, 2013: 18).

According to Nautilus CEO Mike Johnston, one real advantage of sea-floor mineral extraction of this nature is the absence of landowners. This means that, compared to land-based mining projects, there are relatively few ownership and environmental challenges, especially from First Nations peoples. Still, financial, political and operational challenges can arise. The biggest roadblock so far for Nautilus has been a dispute with the Papua New Guinea (PNG) government, which is a co-investor in the project. In 2011, things looked quite promising. The company had secured substantial financing and had a deep-sea mining lease and environment permit in hand. The custom manufacture of production tools was progressing well. Then, in 2012, a dispute with the PNG government arose, halting work on Solwara 1. Speculation in the mining industry is that the government wanted a larger financial share in the project. Other sources suggest that the company was asking PNG for $30 million, a request that had been turned down. Pressure from conservationists is also cited as a factor. Nautilus itself blames a 'rogue trader with a history of questionable actions' who announced to the press that he intended to acquire the company (Nautilus Minerals, 2013). Finally, in April 2014, the company announced that it had renegotiated the deal, with PNG now taking a 15% stake in the project with an option to boost its stake to 30% in return for contributing $120 million towards the costs of the operation (Koven, 2014; Shukman, 2014).

Box 1.2 'Flammable Ice'

The dark horse in the new mining 'frontier' is *methane hydrates* – reserves of natural gas trapped in ice-like form[11] on the seabed. The energy potential of these methane hydrates is enormous, possibly as much as 10 times the entire recoverable natural gas supply globally (Ramirez-Llodra et al., 2011: 13–14). Some estimates indicate that the reserves of methane hydrates in the Nankai Trough within Japan's territorial waters off the nation's central coastline could produce a 100-year supply of natural gas (JOGMEC, 2014).

It tells us something, perhaps, that methane hydrates figure significantly in the first season (2012) of the revival of *Dallas*, the iconic prime-time soap opera that originally ran on American television from 1978 to 1991. In the plot-line, Christopher Ewing (generally a good guy) is attempting to finance and launch an experimental pilot project to extract the volatile gas hydrates from beneath the sea floor. This is contrasted to the conventional, environmentally destructive oil-drilling activities of his rival and cousin John Ross Ewing (a villain). In the real world, pilot plants have been constructed to test extraction technologies. An international joint research team including Japan has obtained successful results in the experimental production of methane gas by injecting hot water into a borehole in the Mackenzie Delta in the Canadian Arctic but 'it remains unclear whether methane gas can be safely or economically extracted from gas hydrate resources in a useable form' (JOGMEC, 2014: 14). However, the technical difficulties associated with tapping this 'flammable ice' or 'burnable ice' suggest that most industrial countries 'are unlikely to invest in the technologies needed to harvest hydrates efficiently', at least as long as relatively cheap oil and gas remain available (Suess et al., 2007). Until then, Robert Monroe's (2005: 13) description of hydrates as 'phantoms from Earth's last frontier preparing to introduce themselves to us in one fashion or another' is probably more or less accurate.

appreciate why and when certain developments occurred. At this point, as befits a Reagan Republican during the late Cold War, Kemp advocates for the aggressive development of American space technology and ocean engineering, for the acceleration of the nation's investments in maritime oil, gas and mineral exploration, and for fuller exploitation of its extensive fishing areas. Although dated, his overview of the relationship between geopolitics and remote resource frontiers is useful in understanding the current state of our deep oceans.

The Oceanic Frontiers narrative identifies a long tradition of exploration and discovery extending all the way back to the epic voyages of Columbus, Magellan and da Gama in the fifteenth and sixteenth centuries. Citing the examples of the opening of the New World, the Cape route and the American West, Kemp (1981: 115) observes that, historically, the exploitation of new frontiers has had a major impact upon the geopolitical perspectives of states, even to the point of changing the shape of international relations. Geopolitics on the oceanic frontier, in this view, is ultimately driven by commercial interest and framed within a quest for human progress, to be achieved through boldness of purpose, technological innovation and scientific inquiry.

This is nicely illustrated by a recent article in the *China Daily* describing an expedition by the manned deep-sea submersible *Jiaolong* in search of iron-manganese deposits in the South China Sea.[12] The refined metals from the deposits, Jin Jiancai, Secretary General of COMRA, told the newspaper, 'will help the country meet the increasing demand for mineral resources during its rapid economic development'. At the same time, this exploratory mission was framed as something more wondrous and scientifically important than simply breaking off deposits from the '*Jiaolong* Seamount' using a robotic arm. 'I will never forget my experience in the deep sea', Li Xinzheng, a biologist who was on board the submersible, told the *Science and Technology Daily*. Not only was the discovery of large-scale mineral deposits exciting, but 'he was also struck by the size of the deep-sea world and its expansive population of strange species, most of which he had never seen before' (*China Daily*, 2013). It is this sense of discovery of new scientific and technological worlds that elevates the Oceanic Frontiers narrative to something more substantial than simply a story about economic competition and deep-sea exploitation.

2
Governing the Abyss: Sharing the Commons

As World War II wound down, US President Franklin Roosevelt was searching for fresh ways to bankroll the nation's economic recovery and growth. Under pressure from the big American oil and gas companies, which were especially eager to drill offshore in the Gulf of Mexico, FDR and his successor, Harry Truman, moved unilaterally to assert jurisdiction over the resources of the continental shelf in 1945. For the Truman Democrats this seemed like a doubly profitable opportunity both to secure political campaign contributions and to tap into new sources of revenue. And indeed it was: during the second half of the twentieth century, oil and gas drilling generated more than a trillion dollars for the oil industry and over $125 billion for the US federal government in offshore oil and gas royalties and lease sales (Helvarg, 2006). By 1964 one sixth of the total production of oil and gas worldwide came from offshore wells (Gullion, 1968: 2).

The 'Truman Doctrine', or 'Truman Proclamation' as it became known, unilaterally extended US jurisdiction over all natural resources of the subsoil and seabed of the continental shelf contiguous to the coasts of the United States,[1] an area encompassing 700,000 square miles. Wolfgang Friedmann (1971: 3–4) characterizes the Truman Proclamation as 'the starting point of a new era in the role of the oceanbed', a trigger that spurred 'a series of rapidly expanding and accelerating claims to exclusive control over the continental shelf'.

This is a view shared by Martin Glassner. While it was quite moderate, he notes, compared with other countries' subsequent maritime claims, the Truman Proclamation was 'explosive' insofar as 'it call[ed] to the attention of the world that there was something of great value out there besides fish, and that nothing in international law or elsewhere prevented a coastal state from claiming it' (Glassner, 1990: 6). Soon, other nations emulated and even exceeded the scope of American claims. For example, in 1946, Argentina went so far as to declare an 'epicontinental sea', comprising sovereignty not only over the continental shelf, but also over the water column above. By 1973, 66 countries had claimed a 12-nautical-mile territorial sea limit, 15 others claimed between 4 and 10 nautical miles, while some others claimed 200 nautical miles or more (Tuerk, 2012: 13). With individual nations arbitrarily drawing their own boundaries, the situation was becoming chaotic.

In fact, the maritime legal code[2] had not been significantly amended for more than 450 years. Since the seventeenth century, the world had more or less subscribed to the so-called 'cannon-shot' rule[3] whereby a nation's rights and jurisdictions over the oceans were limited to a narrow belt of sea adjacent to its coastline, generally set at 3 nautical miles. Now, this rule of thumb was becoming increasingly impractical. Not only were there proliferating disagreements over offshore drilling, but long-distance fishing fleets from industrialized countries, having exhausted fishing grounds adjacent to their own shores, were increasingly ranging far afield, 'invading' the coastal waters of their Southern neighbours (Tuerk, 2012: 8–10). For example, far-ranging tuna boats that ventured into waters claimed by several nations on the west coast of South America were impounded and only released on the payment of a 'ransom' (Wenk, 1972: 254). Similarly, in the 1950s, and again in the early 1970s, a series of confrontations between Iceland and the United Kingdom (known as the 'Cod Wars') flared up in the North Atlantic Ocean over fishing rights.

Mounting concern led to pleas from many within the international community to radically overhaul the existing rules and structures of ocean governance. It took nearly three decades, but this call for the reform of ocean governance was finally realized in the signing of the United Nations Convention on the Law of the Sea (LOSC).[4] The LOSC is the centrepiece of a powerful and continuing narrative about deep-sea geopolitics that I have called 'Governing the Abyss'. According to this storyline, the only way to bring order and protection to an unregulated maritime frontier is to adopt a universal legal regime, whereby the high seas and the deep oceans come under tighter supervision and control of the nations of the world. This is imagined as an ongoing project in which the gains achieved under the LOSC will be extended both to new areas of the deep ocean (e.g. hydrothermal vent sites) and to novel types of underwater activities (e.g. bio-prospecting, deep-sea tourism).

Two Opposing Doctrines

As Helmut Tuerk (2012: 5) points out, most scholarly discussions of who controls the ocean begin with the interplay between two opposing legal doctrines, commonly described by their Latin names *mare clausum* and *mare liberum*. 'The ascendancy of one doctrine over another during any particular historical period,' he observes, 'has tended to reflect the interests of the predominant powers of the day.'

Mare clausum refers to the right of individual rulers and/or nations to assert unchallenged dominion over the sea. This directly contradicted traditional religious doctrine, which stipulated that only Almighty God holds sway over the oceans. According to the famous (and probably apocryphal) story, sitting on his throne in the roiling surf, King Canute (Cnut), the Viking who ruled over England and most of present-day Scandinavia in the eleventh century, commanded the waves to stop. When this did not happen, he sagely instructed his retinue, 'There is only one King who is all powerful and it is God who rules the sea.' Alas, not all rulers were as thoughtful or religiously inclined as Canute. For example, starting in 1269, the newly ascendant mercantile city state of Venice asserted dominion over the entire Adriatic Sea and began charging tolls from all vessels (Buck, 1998: 76). Venice's sovereignty over the sea was recognized by several other European powers and by the Pope, who thereafter faithfully sent his *nuncio* each year to a festival held on Ascension Day in the Venetian harbour channel of Lido (Russell, 2010: 6–7). Later on (1493), Alexander VI, one of the notorious Borgia popes, issued a decree ceding authority to Spain and Portugal over all the 'newly discovered world' stretching from the North Pole to the South Pole. Such declarations, 'enforced by powerful trading leagues, naval policing, or sanctioned by the "international church", established a widespread regime of acceptance of the principle of national control over maritime resources and activities in the defined areas of the oceans' (Roots, 1986: 6–7).

It was not until 1609 when the Dutch jurist and scholar Hugo Grotius published his famous treatise *Mare liberum*[5] that the principle of the sovereign seas was effectively challenged. Citing God's exclusive dominion over nature, Grotius declared the sea common to all *(res communis)*. The seas, he says, represent a residual form of the ancient commons and one that in fact predates the invention of the state. Kathryn Milun (2011: 104) points out that this conveniently circumvented the real landed commons of pre-modern feudal Europe in favour of 'an imaginary description of commons from a "mythic" age, a golden period of pre-state commons that he derived from Greek and Latin mythology'. Consistent with this alternative paradigm, neither the oceans nor their fisheries can be privately owned nor legally appropriated by the state.[6] Commercial shipping, international trade and navigation on the high seas were to be fully protected. Not surprisingly, this appealed enormously to England and Holland, both rising naval powers of the era which opposed monopolistic maritime claims by rivals Spain and Portugal. Grotius' essay, which established the principle of open seas, readily won the backing of Queen Elizabeth I and her advisers[7] and thereafter became a principle of customary international law. This doctrine held because strictures against appropriation of the seas had a limited scope and definition: referring primarily to freedom of navigation, applying mostly to coastal waters and possessing seemingly little relevance to the exploitation of the living resources of the sea (namely fishing), which were considered to be abundant. For all intents and purposes, 'there was no law governing ocean spaces as such' (Tuerk, 2012: 8).

To be sure, *mare liberum* was vigorously challenged by jurists of the day. In his 1635 treatise *Mare clausum* ('Closed Seas'), commissioned by King James I in defence of the British seizure of Dutch cargoes off the coast of Greenland, the English legal scholar John Selden argued that the seas were susceptible to legitimate enclosure and could therefore be lawfully possessed by states (Milun, 2011: 87).

However, Grotius' doctrine more or less persisted – although the limits of territorial seas were regularly disputed – until the Truman Proclamation provoked a tsunami of escalating and 'extensive claims of national jurisdiction' in coastal waters. This led to calls 'to restore order and coherence in an increasingly chaotic situation' (Cicin-Sain and Knecht, 2000: 34). Alan Beesley (2004), a Canadian lawyer who served as chair of the Conference Drafting Committee at UNCLOS III, describes the Law of the Sea in the mid-1960s as 'approaching anarchy'. Beesley notes an escalating number of fisheries and boundaries disputes between developed states and newly independent countries that 'began to challenge the strictures of the past, which they had no hand in developing'. The advent of new technology, particularly factory trawlers and supertankers, drove this process. While he obviously could not have been able to foresee these events in the 1600s, nevertheless the time had come for Grotius to be 'defrocked'.

Pardo's Proposal

Given this increasingly turbulent situation, pressure began to build for a new consensus on the Law of the Sea. One novel and, as it turned out, extremely influential proposal came from Arvid Pardo, Ambassador of Malta to the United Nations. Coming from an island surrounded by illegal fishing fleets eager to exploit the resources of the Mediterranean, he was sensitive to 'the intensifying exploitation of the riches of the continental shelves, notably fish and petroleum' (Glassner, 1990: 10). Pardo was one of the first diplomats of his day to recognize that the seabed, most of which was beyond the limits of national jurisdiction, contained a wealth of untapped resources. Although oil companies were eager to drill in the shallow waters of the continental shelf in the aftermath of World War II (see above), there was virtually no sustained interest in the deep, other than as a support for submarine pipes and cables. 'As late as 1956,' Pardo (1968) observed, 'it was possible [for the International Law Commission] to state that with regard to the ocean floor that apart from the case of exploitation or exploration of the soil or subsoil of a continental shelf . . . such exploitation had not yet assumed sufficient practical importance to justify special regulation.' Yet, a decade later, this was all changing quickly, in no small way thanks to the findings reported by drilling ships such as the *Glomar Challenger* (see Chapter 1). By the 1960s, it was being estimated that a wealth of cobalt, copper, manganese and nickel existed on the deep seabed – an estimated half a trillion tons of manganese nodules alone (Tuerk, 2012: 32).

Pardo concluded that such resources must be declared the 'common heritage of [hu]mankind', not subject to national appropriation, and reserved exclusively for peaceful purposes. Furthermore, he urged that a portion of the revenues derived from the economic exploitation of the seabed be used to bankroll a fund that would help close the gap between rich and poor nations (Woo, 1999). His proposal greatly appealed to 'developing' countries, which were already alarmed at illegal fishing and feared losing out in any unregulated rush for deep-ocean resources. Not only are many of these nations landlocked, they simply do not possess the financial wherewithal to engage in deep-sea exploration and exploitation. The 'common heritage' concept offered less affluent nations in the international community the prospect of the equitable sharing of the benefits accruing from the exploitation of this readily accessible 'fortune on the seabed'.

Pardo presented his proposal in a three-hour speech at the First Committee of the United Nations General Assembly on 1 November 1967, provoking an immediate and notable reaction.[8] Seyom Brown and his co-authors (1977: 74) argue that Pardo instantly turned the terms of the growing international dialogue around. The phrase 'common heritage of [hu]mankind' (CHM) became the rallying cry of the advocates of international control or regulation of the deep seabed by a newly created international organization or agency (Payoyo, 1997: 366). Whereas previously the notion of common international property in ocean resources was used to justify open access and free use by all members of the international community, Pardo insisted that 'the international community's common ownership of the resources of the deep seabed meant that the international community, acting through international institutions, should govern the exploitation of the resources and reap the rewards, and that any exploitation of the deep seabed not authorized by the international community was illegitimate.'

Peter Payoyo argues that the boldness of the Maltese agenda item, and Ambassador Pardo's address, should not be underestimated. In particular, the phrase used as part of its unwieldy title, 'sea-bed and ocean floor underlying the seas beyond the limits of present national jurisdiction', was 'not at all an innocuous description in oceanography, but a highly explosive political hypothesis' (Payoyo, 1997: 168).

As Maria Gavouneli (2007: 136) observes, Pardo's idea 'fit perfectly within the ideological environment of its era'. After World War II there was a major shift in the global economy towards a (neo)liberal market system that largely replaced the former system of colonialism in Africa and most of Asia. Paul Rogers (2000: 80–1) contends that this delivered economic growth, but at the expense of economic and social justice. The end result was the success of the few at the expense of the many, such that socioeconomic disparities grew and a substantial proportion of the world's population experienced extreme poverty and marginalization. During the early to mid-1970s, there were calls at the United Nations and other global forums for a 'New International Economic Order' (NIEO)[9] that would reject the traditional market system, redress income gaps between nations and reduce the influence of multinational organizations in the world economy. This collective vision for the future played out at the UNCLOS III negotiations, especially with regard to seabed issues. Jack Barkenbus (1979: 165) asks why the seabed should have become a prime battle-ground for achieving a new international order, given the low profile of manganese nodules. The answer, he says, is that this is primarily a symbolic issue where nations of the South can adopt a unified position without injuring the interests of any single country, much in the same way as the European Parliament has long been inclined to act in concert to sanction the Canadian seal hunt and its products. More pragmatically, it might have been easier to visualize and manage, because, unlike fish, the seabed did not appear to migrate.

The LOSC (United Nations Law of the Sea Convention)

During this era, there was mounting pressure to forge a new international maritime treaty. Writing in 1968, Louis Henkin, professor of international law and diplomacy at Columbia University and a former State Department official, observed, 'Proposals for a new law have been cropping up with increasing frequency, differing widely in basic philosophy, in scope, and in the care and detail with which they have been prepared' (Henkin, 1968: 83). These proposals offered four differing paths in the development of international authority over the oceans: a path leading to the barest minimum of international rules; a path leading through a series of bilateral agreements; a path that would terminate in vesting a measure of control in some kind of international organization; and a path towards the actual ownership of ocean space and resources by an international organization. The first two paths here further the interests of advanced or wealthy nations, while the latter two choices favour the vesting of independent power in international organizations (Gullion, 1968: 8).

Various attempts during the 1950s and 1960s to establish a new international order of the oceans fell short. The first two UN conferences on the Law of the Sea (UNCLOS I and II), convened in 1958 and 1960, did not succeed in resolving the increasingly urgent problems of ocean management, failing to produce an agreement on the issue of the breadth of the territorial sea and fishery limits (Egede and Sutch, 2013: 309; Levering and Levering, 1999: 3). On the basis of extensive research by the International Law Commission, the 1958 Geneva Convention on the Continental Shelf, produced at UNCLOS I, did give coastal nations sovereign rights to their continental shelves out to a water depth of 200 metres or 'where technology can reach'. Edmund Gullion (1968: 5) notes that the final phrase here (known as the 'exploitability clause') 'leaves much to be desired, for it gives those states bordering the oceans an opportunity to claim more and more of the seabed, further inhibiting other uses of the sea by other nations'. O. P. Sharma, a former Senior Deputy Director of the International Maritime Organization, agrees with Gullion's assessment: 'Seen in retrospect, the exploitability criterion [clause] was a loophole which triggered a strong criticism of the above definition since exploitation of nodules from the deep ocean floor at depths of over 3,000 metres was now possible and it was apparent that on this basis, all seabed resources could legally come under the creeping jurisdiction of coastal States' (Sharma, 2009: 174).

Then, in 1970, inspired by Arvid Pardo's proposal, the UN General Assembly unanimously adopted a 'Declaration of Principles Governing the Seabed and the Ocean Floor and the Subsoil Thereof, Beyond the Limits of National Jurisdiction'. This 'Declaration of Principles' used the 'common heritage' language. The General Assembly also convened a Third United Nations Conference on the Law of the Sea, to be started within three years.

Alas, negotiations dragged on for nine years before the United Nations Convention on the Law of the Sea was finally adopted in December 1982 in Montego Bay, Jamaica. As it happens, this coincided with Antarctic negotiations over fishing and then minerals which started in 1982. Edward Miles (1998: 5–6) compares UNCLOS III to a large snake, moving slowly through time with many twists and turns and phases within phases, stalling at times and 'moving forward (or sideways) again only after the leadership saw potential failure looming large'. But the snake then hibernated; the ratification process languished for a further decade, with the issue of commercial manganese nodule mining posing a particular problem. Finally, after a process of informal consultations[10] initiated by the Secretary-General of the United Nations designed to make Part XI of the Convention more universally acceptable, an 'Implementation Agreement of Part XI of the Convention' entered into force on 16 November 1994 when the necessary number of ratifications was reached (Borgese, 1998: 112).

Despite being part of the UNCLOS III negotiations, the United States has yet to ratify the Convention. In a 'Statement on United States Oceans Policy' released on 10 March 1983, President Ronald Reagan explained,

> Last July, I announced that the United States will not sign the United Nations Law of the Sea Convention that was opened for signature on December 10. We have taken this step because several major problems in the Convention's deep seabed mining provisions are contrary to the interests and principles of industrialized nations and would not help attain the aspirations of developing countries.

A decade later (1994), during the Clinton presidency, the Convention and the accompanying Implementation Agreement reached the Senate for ratification as demanded by the US Constitution, only to stall there indefinitely, despite presidential support from Clinton onwards. While there are multiple interest groups in the United States that favour accession to the Convention, the issue does not resonate very widely or strongly with the American electorate. As a result, the treaty has twice successfully proceeded through the Senate Foreign Relations Committee, only to expire on the agenda before making it to a scheduled vote in the full Senate (Duff, 2014: 753).

Writing at the half-way mark of the UNCLOS III talks, Pardo (1978: 10) claimed that the main obstacle to progress at the conference was 'the vastness, importance, and complexity of the subject matter; the conflicting interests of States; and the difficulty of elaborating an effective and efficient international regime for the seabed beyond national jurisdiction . . . which can equitably balance the interests of developed and developing countries'. Echoing Pardo's statement, there are several explanations for the glacial pace of negotiations at UNCLOS III. First of all, this was undoubtedly a complex and comprehensive task, involving nothing less than a total reworking of the Law of the Sea. It covered a wide range of issues, including piracy, sea-lane passage and respect for submarine cables and pipelines. The most contentious question concerned limits to the continental shelf and jurisdiction over the ocean floor beyond the shelf, but there were a proliferating number of controversial problems: the EEZ concept; straits used for international navigation; archipelagoes; islands; scientific research; and ship-generated pollution (Miles, 1998: 17).

Second, there were multiple divisions among the participating nations and a series of shifting coalitions over the nine years of negotiations. Edward Miles, who has written what is probably the most comprehensive book on the structure and dynamics of the decision process at UNCLOS III, identifies two key overlapping dimensions to the conflicts that arose in the conference: the first pitted developing states in the South against advanced industrial countries in the North, while the second set all landlocked and geographically disadvantaged countries against those big maritime states that stood to gain the most from the EEZ concept.

The North/South confrontation was at its most extreme in the Committee I deliberations about the seabed, where the 20 to 30 countries that actually had substantive issues at stake and possessed the capability to exploit the deep seabed were aligned against the remaining 100 or so delegations that did not and preferred to engage in symbolic politics (Miles, 1998: 20–1, 24). Countries most likely to engage in deep-sea mining in the near future were primarily interested in creating an 'orderly gold rush' (Payoyo, 1997: 366) through establishing an international authority that would act in the capacity of a claims registry. On their part, developing countries wanted to engineer an agreement that would provide them with revenues from seabed mining and, optimally, establish an international agency that would actually be the mining operator on their behalf (Buck, 1998: 88). Payoyo (1997: 366–7) conceives of this as two competing trajectories or contradictory visions of internationalization. One proposed that an international seabed agency should assume the role of a vanguard in the promotion of a new set of supranational norms and global moral values. The other sought to create a seabed regulatory mechanism that would preserve and justify an international legal order governed solely by norms of competition and national interest.

Differences in outlook existed not only among countries, but sometimes also between various departments and agencies within a nation state. During negotiations on UNCLOS

III, the US Defense Department and the Navy looked suspiciously on proposals to extend the breadth of the continental shelf. They feared that the 'creeping jurisdiction' associated with expanding coastal state control would impede military and commercial navigation and severely limit their ability to place submarine-tracking systems on portions of the ocean floor (Levering and Levering, 1999: 48). In fact, the military was willing to accept a compromise (Laursen, 1982). By contrast, officials at the Departments of the Treasury and Interior, strongly supported by most big oil companies, generally supported changes in the international Law of the Sea allowing coastal states (and especially the United States) to control all recoverable energy resources under the ocean floor, and to license prospective deep-seabed miners (Laursen, 1982). They were horrified by the prospect of control over the world's oceans being assigned to an international authority.

In similar fashion, Japanese participation in UNCLOS III was a complex affair because it represented diverse and often conflicting private and bureaucratic interests. Haruhiro Fukui (1984: 25) reports, 'Before every UNCLOS session, thorough consultations were held between representatives of the Foreign Ministry office and other ministries and agencies. Agreement was often reached only with great difficulty at the cost of more than a month of inter-ministry negotiations.' As the negotiations continued, year after year, most bureaucratic stakeholders began to lose interest, allowing the Foreign Ministry to monopolize the right to speak officially for the Japanese government.

In light of these contested positions, why did consensus finally emerge? One answer is that failure simply was not an option because the stakes were too high. That is, if agreement was not reached, the spectre of chaos loomed. On several occasions, it appeared that the talks were close to going up in flames, only to revive at the last moment. Miles (1998: 497) confirms this: 'It must also be said that the conference tended to make significant progress only after the glimpse of potential failure.'

Another explanation points to the momentum generated by the 1972 Stockholm Conference (the United Nations Conference on the Human Environment), where the 'common heritage of [hu]mankind' principle first featured (Pease, 2008: 230–1). Others have pointed to the contribution of social movement activists. According to one version, the Neptune Group, a collaboration between the Ocean Educational Project and the United Methodist Law of the Sea Project, both of which were deeply committed to promoting peace and international cooperation through world governance, 'played a crucial role on UNCLOS, acting as an "honest broker" between the negotiating states' (Flint, 2011: 165). The two key personalities here were said to be Lee Kimball and Miriam Levering. The Neptune Group made three key contributions: organizing seminars for delegates; researching technical issues relevant to debates; and publishing a newspaper to help circulate ideas and information. Ralph Levering (1997: 231) contrasts these efforts to be helpful and reasonable with the more idealistic and strident 'advocacy' style of other larger and better-known social movement organizations, an approach that 'proved ineffective and unpopular with delegates, who disliked being lectured on what the treaty ideally should contain'.

In both his 1997 article and in the book co-authored (after her death) with his mother Miriam, Levering, an American history professor, comments negatively on the efforts of the late Elisabeth Mann Borgese, founder of the International Ocean Institute (IOI), head of the maritime NGO *Pacem in Maribus*, a founding member of the Club of Rome and the daughter of the famed novelist Thomas Mann. Borgese, the Leverings charge, was an ivory tower idealist who tactlessly hectored delegates to UNCLOS III, notably on her proposal to share oil and gas revenues from near-shore drilling with developing nations (Levering and Levering, 1999: 33). According to Betsy Baker (2012: 26–7, 33), a Vermont legal scholar who has done archival research on Borgese's activities leading up to UNCLOS III, the Leverings' account 'lacks critical perspective in places', but any definitive account of Borgese's influence, and that of the IOI, 'requires further study'.

Not surprisingly, the NGOs summarily dismissed by the Leverings offer a more positive assessment of their own accomplishments. Notably, the IOI, which acquired observer status to UNCLOS III in 1974, and its co-founder Elisabeth Mann Borgese, claim to have contributed positively by 'providing an important forum for individuals involved in UNCLOS III to exchange and test ideas that would help inform the treaty that eventually emerged from the negotiations' (Baker, 2012: 34).

Anne Simon (1984: 127–8) attributes the breakthrough that produced a historic agreement on deep-sea mineral resources to the extraordinary efforts of two negotiators, Paul Bamela Engo and Henry Kissinger. Simon credits Engo, a judge and ambassador from Cameroon who chaired Committee I,[11] with using his strong, upbeat personality to break a logjam in negotiations and broker a compromise between the big industrial nations and the 'Group of 77'. It was, she gushes, 'a triumph for the Cameroon diplomat'. Edward Miles (1998: 54) offers a more balanced explanation. In the first phase of the Conference, administrative control over the course of negotiations was tenuous, fragmentation became a chronic problem and compromise seemed elusive. To counter this and move negotiations along, committee chairs were given greater latitude to act on their own. Engo evidently took full advantage of these increased powers in order to make unilateral changes, often without the agreement of all the parties involved. This led to considerable conflict within Committee I, notably with Christopher Pinto,[12] the Sri Lankan ambassador to Germany, who chaired the Working Group. Miles suggests that Engo's arbitrary style became counterproductive and gives greater credit for reaching agreement to the efforts of a stable of skilful mediators, notably Tommy Koh of Singapore, who was elected president of the Conference in March 1981 after the death of Hamilton Amerasinghe, the first president.

US Secretary of State Henry Kissinger moved negotiations along within Committee I when they seemed to be deadlocked (Simon, 1984: 127–8). The so-called 'Kissinger Compromise' not only offered some new concessions from the United States but it was also backed up by an explicit threat: 'If the deep seabeds are not subject to international agreement the US can and will proceed to explore and mine on its own' (Miles, 1998: 219). In the end, the United States did go it alone, but Kissinger had already pressured the Conference into forging a consensus. Jack Barkenbus (1979: 158) disagrees with this interpretation. While acknowledging that

Kissinger's message to foreign delegates was a masterful example of offering carrots in one hand (a temporary limit on seabed mineral production) while holding a stick in the other (the implied threat to move forward unilaterally if a seabed treaty was not forthcoming), he concludes that 'the impact of Kissinger's entrance into UNCLOS negotiations was negligible', especially after Gerald Ford was defeated in the 1976 presidential election and a new Secretary of State was appointed.

Key Principles and Provisions Relating to the Deep Ocean

While it is far from perfect, the LOSC nevertheless represents a defining moment in the evolution of the Law of the Sea. Scott Allen (1996: 21) says its chief legacy 'has been the codification of Selden over Grotius, of *mare clausum* over *mare liberum*'. Tullio Scovazzi (2013: 555) calls the LOSC 'a cornerstone in the field of codification of international law' and says that it is 'rightly qualified as a constitution for the ocean'. Maria Gavouneli (2006: 205) goes a step further. The LOSC, she suggests, is 'more than a constitution'. Rather, it 'provides a comprehensive regulatory regime for all matters maritime' and 'remains the one example of a successful integral document which has come to prevail over any other expression of State power by the sheer force of its existence'. There are three unique and defining elements of the LOSC: the Exclusive Economic Zone, the 'common heritage of [hu]mankind' principle and the International Seabed Authority.

The EEZ (Exclusive Economic Zone)

Adalberto Vallega (1992: 73) calls the EEZ, established by the 1982 Convention, 'the most intriguing process involving the sea and also the main tool for extending the space in which national interests can be pursued'. By the late 1990s, EEZs accounted for an estimated 8% of the earth's surface and 90% of the world's fish catch (Soares, 1998: 59). The EEZ is the product of a compromise reached between the majority of coastal states, mostly developing countries, and the main maritime powers. The former desired protection from intrusion into their territorial waters by factory fishing vessels from abroad, while the latter wanted to preserve the freedom of the seas, particularly as it applies to navigation (Vukas, 2006: 251). The solution was to create a special category of marine area beyond the outer limits of the territorial sea and equip it with a unique legal status.

O. P. Sharma (2009: 130–1) gives the credit for formally articulating and sponsoring a proposal on the EEZ to Frank Njenga of Kenya. Njenga pointed out that in 1970 the developed countries, with less than a third of the world's population, had taken 60% of the world catch of fish, while only 40% had gone to the developing countries. A new, more equal system was badly needed which would provide more freedom of opportunity. Although it had precursors, nevertheless, the EEZ, Sharma (2009: 131) argues, is 'a radical experiment in international law'.

According to Part VI of the LOSC, the EEZ is a legally designated sea zone extending from the coast of a state outward for a distance of 200 nautical miles. Coastal states also have jurisdiction over continental shelves that extend beyond 200 nautical miles. Within this zone, the state has jurisdiction over the exploration and use of resources. Foreign fishing fleets may operate here, but subject to the regulation of the coastal state. EEZs are mixed legal jurisdictions based on 'sovereign rights', as opposed to sovereignty (McConnell, 2011: 222). In other words, national states cannot exercise the full sovereignty that they enjoy in their home waters, but nonetheless possess certain legally guaranteed rights. Although the EEZ was not specifically invented with the deep ocean in mind, it has become the site for an increasing volume of activity involving deep-ocean resource exploration and extraction, as well as a testing space for technology that might then be used in the deep.

'Common Heritage of [Hu]mankind'

It is fair to state, I think, that the most revolutionary and controversial element in the 'new order of the oceans' (Portecovo, 1986) was the CHM concept. This constitutes nothing less than 'the fundamental principle on which the deep seabed mining regime is based' (Tuerk, 2012: 44).

According to Bernardo Zuleta, an Undersecretary-General at the United Nations and Special Representative to UNCLOS III, Arvid Pardo did not invent the concept of the CHM. Rather, the idea had a long provenance, dating from French jurist Albert Geoffre de Lapradelle (1871–1955) and diplomat Prince Wan Waithayakon (1891–1976), a one-time foreign minister of Thailand (Simon, 1984: 126). Earlier, in 1820, the South American poet and jurist Andrès Bello had written that there were areas of the planet which should be set apart in common for the use of all people: he described this as an 'indivisible common patrimony' (Tuerk, 2012: 31).

When Pardo featured it in his 1967 UN speech, the concept was in the air, although it meant different things to different people. In 1966, US President Lyndon Johnson (1967) told those gathered for the commissioning of a research vessel, 'Under no circumstances, we believe, must we ever allow the prospects of rich harvest and mineral wealth to create a new form of colonial competition among the maritime nations. We must insure that the deep seas and the ocean bottoms are, and remain, the legacy of all human beings.' In the United States, Johnson's speech[13] received widespread press coverage and favourable comment (Wenk, 1972: 258).

Susan Buck notes that support for the CHM principle in the 1960s and 1970s sprung from two realizations in the international community, especially the developing nations. First, valuable resource stocks such as certain fisheries were close to exhaustion and the 'have not' nations wanted to ensure that these resources would still be around for them to use. Second, these countries realized that they would be disadvantaged by the first-come-first-served rule in resource realms such as deep-seabed mining. Thus, CHM was 'an assertion of their right to participate in exploitation and a moral claim to the development assistance needed for participation' (Buck, 1998: 29).

The CHM concept signalled a major shift in the geopolitics of the oceans. Jill Stuart (2009: 15) describes the 'common heritage' principle that developed for the high seas as the 'embodiment' of a shift from the classical (Westphalian) model of sovereignty to a liberal sovereignty model which attempts to distribute resources not according to statehood but rather based on the rights of individuals. 'Common heritage' approaches 'represent the exclusion of right of appropriation; the duty to use resources in the interests of the whole of humanity; and the duty to explore and exploit resources for peaceful purposes' (Stuart, 2009: 15).

In addition to becoming the chief international legal instrument governing the exploitation of seabed resources, the CHM principle describes the conditions under which marine scientific research may be conducted. The freedom of scientists to conduct research varies considerably depending on the area being addressed. According to the general rules of the LOSC, permission to conduct marine scientific research carried out in areas that are under the jurisdiction of the coastal state is freely given, as long as it is undertaken 'exclusively for peaceful purposes' and is 'for the benefit of all [hu]mankind' (LOSC, Article 246, paragraph 3). In the EEZ or on the continental shelf, coastal states are allowed to withhold consent if the project to be carried out 'is of direct significance for the exploration and exploitation of natural resources, whether living or non-living' (LOSC, Article 246, paragraph 5(a)). By contrast, marine areas beyond national jurisdiction, including much of the deep ocean, remain in somewhat of a grey area. Coastal states have no regulatory power here, with little leeway given to any meaningful intervention by the international community (Gavouneli, 2007: 150). At the same time, the communal obligations about peaceful use and common benefit of (hu)mankind still apply. The powers of the International Seabed Authority (see below) to regulate scientific research on the ocean bottom are yet to be fully defined.

Lyle Glowka (1996) pinpoints a fundamental weakness here. The Convention defines neither 'marine scientific research' nor 'benefit of all [hu]mankind'. The former is especially problematic when applied to the search for deep-sea genetic resources. That is, the distinction between marine scientific research and activities such as bio-prospecting that are undertaken purely to uncover commercially useful information and natural resources can be 'blurry' and 'varies with the nature and intent of the activity at issue' (Glowka, 1996: 173). Insofar as marine scientific research on the genetic resources of the ocean beyond national jurisdictions, known as the 'Area',[14] is increasingly risky and expensive, and government funding for research is decreasing, there is greater pressure for researchers to pass along organisms discovered on the seabed to industry as a form of technology transfer. This could result in greater secrecy, thus violating basic scientific norms about the free publication and dissemination of research results. Similar questions have been raised about bio-prospecting in Antarctica.

The International Seabed Authority (ISA)

If the CHM is the guiding principle of the deep-seabed mining regime, the ISA is its chief regulatory mechanism. It is one of three new institutions established at UNCLOS III – the other two are the Commission on the Limits of the Continental Shelf and the International Tribunal for the Law of the Sea (Nandon, 2005: 1). Nilufer Oral (2006: 97) calls the ISA 'one of the major innovations of the LOS Convention', while Alfonso Ascencio and Michael Bliss (2003: 13), legal advisers at the United Nations, characterize the agency as follows,

> The ISA is the institution with the most direct focus on the high seas and deep oceans. It is the only oceans institution with a field of competence exclusively focused on areas beyond national jurisdiction. It is also in a relatively strong regulatory position; the only way in which an actor can undertake mining activity in the Area is by first obtaining ISA authorization.

The ISA became operational in 2011. Its brief is to regulate deep-seabed mining activities, administer resources in the seabed areas and protect the environment for the CHM. Since 2001, the ISA has issued 30 exploration permits for the Pacific, mid-Atlantic and Indian Oceans (International Mining, 2014).

Jack Barkenbus (1979: 103–4) argues that the most crucial and enduring debate in seabed negotiations at UNCLOS III was the question of whether to create a standard international organization having limited, largely technical goals and functions to regulate seabed activities beyond international jurisdiction, or, alternatively, to create a much more powerful and autonomous international organization that would counter the influence and power of public and private mining entities and assure that mineral exploitation will be undertaken for the benefit of all (hu)mankind. The United States and other nations that were actively engaged in seabed mineral exploration favoured the former position, while the Group of 77 preferred the latter. Committee I negotiations at UNCLOS III were deadlocked for so long owing to differences in how the North and South defined the ISA's powers, functions, tasks and internal decision-making structure (Barkenbus, 1979: xii). Which of these options the ISA currently represents is a matter of sharp debate.

On the one hand, there is no doubt that the ISA mandate goes well beyond that of other international regulatory organizations such as the International Civil Aviation Organization. All rights to the resources of the seabed beyond the limits of national jurisdiction are vested in it, a provision that gives the ISA the legal authority to issue permits and contracts for deep-sea mining prospecting and exploration. As administrator of the Area, the ISA is tasked with policing any instances of encroachment and collecting penalties for so doing. Under Article 145 of the LOSC it has the obligation to protect the seabed and ocean floor in the Area from harmful environmental effects, or at least those that pertain to mining activities.

At the same time, there are still plenty of gaps in and restrictions on the ISA's powers. The inability to oversee regulation of hydrothermal vent sites is especially problematic because of the immense wealth of biological diversity to be found. Furthermore, the ISA has not been given jurisdiction over bio-prospecting or bio-discovery – neither term even appears in the text of the LOSC (Gavouneli, 2007: 135–6). While the ISA has the obligation to protect the seabed 'from harmful effects which may arise from activities in the Area' (LOSC, Article 154), this power is left somewhat vague, especially when it comes to pollution generated by activities other than seabed mining.

Deficiencies and Limitations

Fourteen years after his landmark presentation to the United Nations, Arvid Pardo declared the LOSC 'probably the most inequitable treaty that has ever been signed in the world' (Woo, 1999). Given that his concept of the CHM is often cited as the guiding philosophy of the agreement, this seems quite surprising. Pardo had, it seems, become disillusioned because he felt UNCLOS III favoured big maritime states, which managed to maintain the rights to the most accessible underwater resources. Additionally, he described the Convention as falling 'little short of disaster' because it applied only to mineral resources, whereas his original proposal covered all the natural resources, living and non-living, on the international sea floor beyond the 200-nautical-mile limit of coastal state jurisdiction (Gavouneli, 2007: 140–1).

Another high-profile critic of the Law of the Sea is the marine scientist and award-winning author Callum Roberts. Conceived and written in the 1960s and 1970s, the LOSC is badly outdated now, Roberts complains. He is especially upset about the failure of the Convention to create high-seas marine protected areas, which he describes as places off limits to exploitation that represent 'an indispensable building block of our New Deal for the oceans' (Roberts, 2012: 296). The Convention's default position, says Roberts (2012: 331), 'is that all of the seas must be exploited'. Two decades after the Convention was finally put in place, not much seems to have changed. At Rio+20 (United Nations Conference on Sustainable Development, held in Rio de Janeiro in June 2012), an initiative to develop the needed framework for the establishment of marine protected areas on the high seas, a key strategy in enhancing biodiversity conservation and combating industrial fishing, was deferred for at least another two and a half years (Lieberman and Yang, 2013: 86).

While Pardo's and Roberts's assessments seem a bit harsh, nonetheless a number of weaknesses and deficiencies have become apparent. Part XI of the Convention has proven to be a particular lightning rod for discontent. Elisabeth Mann Borgese (1998: 112) summed up the deficiencies here as follows:

> PART XI was fundamentally flawed: shaped by politics and ideological compromise rather than responding to the needs of a modern high-tech undertaking. It was based on certain premises – that manganese nodules were the only

economically interesting resource on the deep-sea-bed; that they were all located in the international Area; that commercial mining would start in the 1980s; that the industrialized states would be the only ones capable of exploring and exploiting these resources, which all turned out to be wrong.

Borgese's critique has two aspects. First there is the oft-made observation that UNCLOS III negotiators were handicapped by the necessity of making laws to govern a commercial activity, deep-sea mining, that had not yet started up; activities such as bio-prospecting or geo-engineering that were not even contemplated in the 1970s; and new environmental impacts such as those from the transfer of ballast water[15] between oceans that the UNCLOS drafters did not anticipate. While this is certainly true, we should not be surprised that the fit between regulation and reality has turned out to be imperfect. As Tullio Scovazzi (2013: 555) points out, 'UNCLOS cannot regulate those activities that its drafters did not intend to regulate for the simple reason that they were not foreseeable in the period when this treaty was being negotiated.' After all, it would be churlish to dismiss the historical importance of Grotius' famous treatise on the grounds that he could not anticipate by 400 years the advent of supertankers or factory fishing vessels. To be sure, the reach and scope of the LOSC has certainly not remained static: regulations on prospecting and exploration for polymetallic sulphides were adopted in 2010 and for cobalt-rich crusts in 2012, while in 2013 the rules governing polymetallic nodules were revised and updated so as to be in sync with the 2010 and 2012 additions (Lodge et al., 2014: 67).

A more substantive criticism, I think, is that some damaging compromises were made, especially in the 1994 Implementation Agreement. Helmut Tuerk (2012: 41) notes the oft-expressed view that the CHM has been given 'a first-class burial'. While it is true, he says, that the 1994 Implementation Agreement preserved and re-affirmed the fundamental principle on which the deep-seabed mining regime is based – that of the CHM – it also significantly changed the original LOSC pact inasmuch as 'commercial concerns had eroded the original redistributionist ideals, shifting the balance between use and distribution in favor of the former' (Tuerk, 2012: 44).

Whereas the developing countries originally insisted that the international organization in charge of mining the seabed (the operational arm of the ISA, known as the 'Enterprise') be the actual mining operator on their behalf, the Implementation Agreement stipulated that an initial mining operation in the zone be a joint venture between the Enterprise and the licensed mining operator (Buck, 1998: 88, 91). In the 1982 agreement, as a condition of receiving approval to undertake projects on the deep seabed, mining firms (referred to in the legal language of the document as the 'Contractor') were compelled to transfer their technology to the Enterprise or to developing countries. In the 1994 Implementation Agreement this was watered down. Now, the Contractor was ascribed a 'general duty of cooperation' to help the Enterprise or developing country to obtain such a technology if the latter was unable to obtain it on the open market or through joint-venture agreements. In a similar fashion, the idea of limiting production from deep-seabed minerals so as to protect land-based producers was modified. In the Agreement, several alternative principles were substituted, prohibiting subsidization of mining activities in the Area by nation states, and disallowing discrimination between minerals derived from the Area and those obtained from other sources (Freestone, 2007: 514). In short, the Implementation Agreement is said to have effectively undermined the normative ambitions of ocean governance reformers, which were that the LOSC was to become an exercise in 'global distributive justice' (Egede and Sutch, 2013: 307).

Another significant concern is that ocean governance remains highly sectoral, meaning that it is patchy, complex and quite uneven when it comes to scope and effectiveness. A particular irritant is the multiplicity of parallel jurisdictions. The Report of the World Commission on the Oceans lists 'multiple international institutions' as one of the chief barriers to good ocean governance. While praising the LOSC as 'a tangible achievement', nevertheless the Report cites the difficulties created by 'treaty congestion' – the proliferation of legal regimes and institutions, each with its own constituency within national government agencies (Soares, 1998: 146).

Consider, for example, the rather tangled issue of the exploration for and exploitation of marine genetic resources (i.e. bio-prospecting) in the deep oceans. Alfonso Ascencio and Michael Bliss (2003: 28) describe the situation as follows: 'A number of relevant institutions do not have a specific focus on oceans and sea-related matters. . . . Further, the mandates of many institutions were established without reference to those other institutions. The result is a patchwork of different institutions, each with a different focus and different programmes of work.'

There are two primary and overlapping governance tools here: the LOSC and the 1992 Convention on Biological Diversity (CBD), entered into force in 1993. The latter provides an international legal framework for the conservation of biological diversity, the sustainable use of its components and the fair and equitable sharing of benefits arising from the utilization of genetic and biological resources (Herber, 2006: 141). To a certain extent the two treaties are complementary and mutually reinforcing. However, the LOSC is anchored by the profits-oriented CHM principle, while the CBD opts for the concept of the 'common concern of humankind' (Gavouneli, 2007: 154–6).

The jurisdictional scope of the CBD is essentially limited to territorial waters and to the EEZs, acknowledging the sovereign rights of states over their own natural resources. This means that bio-prospecting in the deep-seabed segment of the high seas remains virtually unregulated. This is also the case for the high-seas zone of the oceans beyond EEZs but above the deep seabed, which reverts to 'flag state jurisdiction'. However, there are possible caveats. Insofar as the ISA has the obligation under Article 145 of the LOSC to protect the seabed and ocean floor in the Area from harmful environmental effects, the agency may well have standing where potential threats to biodiversity can be demonstrated. Officially, the ISA's powers extend only to mining. However, in some circumstances, mining and bio-prospecting activities could be intertwined: for example, the sampling of biological resources may occur in the course of exploration of mineral deposits (Herber, 2006: 142). Furthermore, some legal scholars have argued that under the CBD member states are required to assume full responsibility for their nationals who are engaging in bio-prospecting, no matter where this occurs, because the 'harvesting' of biological resources takes place offsite in locations that fall under the legal jurisdiction of the state (Gavouneli, 2007: 153–4). Finally, there is a basic contradiction in the LOSC. On the one hand, the agreement puts forward the idea of the CHM. On the other hand, it allows the enlargement of the sea subject to national jurisdiction through provisions such as the extension of the seabed of the EEZ up to the outer edge of the continental margin (Scovazzi, 2013: 556). Thus, the adoption of the EEZ in the LOSC can be interpreted as an example of 'creeping coastal state jurisdiction' challenging the commons/high-seas regime (McConnell, 2011: 226), while fears for a 'creeping common heritage' (Gavouneli, 2007: 141) have been stoked by the creation of centralized regulatory regimes guided by the 'common heritage' principle.

Conclusion

From a policy discourse perspective, the most widely disseminated narrative of deep oceans is what I call Governing the Abyss. Whereas the Oceanic Frontiers narrative is largely economic in intent, and the Sovereignty Games narrative frames global ocean issues in starkly realist political terms, the Governing the Abyss narrative is legal and normative. The tools of international law are strategically deployed here in order to 'protect' the deep from aggressive coastal powers seeking to extend their sphere of influence as well as from rapacious fisheries, energy and mining companies who would exploit ocean resources for commercial profit. However, equally, if not more, important is the goal of cutting 'have not' nations in on the wealth to be generated by the commercial exploitation of underwater resources, most notably through seabed and hydrothermal vent mining projects. Since 1967, when Maltese diplomat Arvid Pardo introduced a proposal in the United Nations General Assembly to replace the principle of the freedom of the seas with the principle of the 'common heritage of [hu]mankind', a regulatory approach has assumed a position at the forefront of the global dialogue over deep oceans.

At the end of World War II, the world's oceans were still divided into four jurisdictional zones: internal waters, the territorial sea, the contiguous zone and the high seas. In 1986, four years after the LOSC was initially adopted, five more zones had been added: the continental shelf, the exclusive fishing zone, the EEZ, archipelagic waters and the Area beyond the limits of national jurisdiction (Brown, 1986: 15).

The Governing the Abyss narrative dictates that removing the deep ocean from the jurisdiction of nation states and re-assigning it to newly created, transnational governance structures is the only effective way of regulating and redistributing the resources that abound in the untamed frontier of the deep. Among the eight recommendations for action of the 2014 Global Ocean Commission is the necessity of drafting a new agreement under the LOSC that would impose international governance on a significant portion of the world's oceans that lie outside national jurisdiction. The Commission urges the creation of a Global Ocean Accountability Board whose responsibility it would be to monitor and assess whether sufficient progress is being made towards reversing the degradation and regeneration of the global ocean and securing effective and equitable governance. Additionally, the Commission recommends the appointment of a Special Representative of the Secretary-General for the Ocean with overall responsibility for the coordination of all matters relating to the oceans and the Law of the Sea within the UN system.

The Commission is but one among many 'friends of the ocean' to conclude that the looming threat to the global marine commons can only be averted by creating an integrated 'super-agency' to oversee international action on the seas. The Independent World Commission on the Oceans recommends the establishment of a World Ocean Affairs Observatory that would 'independently monitor the system of ocean governance' and 'exercise, on a continuous basis, an external watch on ocean affairs' (Soares, 1998: 161). Elisabeth Mann Borgese takes this one step further, calling 'for the creation of a new world order for the ocean, which would serve as a model for a new world order to follow' (Allen,

1996: 26). Not surprisingly, this global governance talk does not sit well with all of the parties involved in shaping the future of deep oceans. In particular, it plays into the hands of opponents in the US Senate to ratification of the LOSC, who have long argued that the real agenda of the environmental movement is to wrench sovereignty away from nation states.

3
Sovereignty Games: Claiming the Commons

When Arvid Pardo delivered his path-breaking three-hour speech to the United Nations in 1967 (see Chapter 2), the remote seabed with its treasures was perceived not only as an economic Eldorado, but equally as 'a prized object upon which national power and prestige might be projected' (Payoyo, 1997: 169). That is, rather than a resource frontier to be conquered for the purpose of mineral and hydrocarbon exploitation, it was regarded as a territorial frontier that must be secured for political and military purposes. For example, seamounts were thought to be ideal sites for military activities such as the emplacement of weapon systems or the construction of undersea stations. It is worth recalling, says Peter Payoyo (1997: 170, n. 131), that the agenda item proposed by Pardo on behalf of Malta was eventually assigned to the First (Political) Committee of the UN General Assembly rather than to its Economic or Legal Committee.

This introduces our third narrative, Sovereignty Games, which frames the deep ocean primarily from the twin vantage points of political ambition and national security. Typically, a 2007 dispatch in the UK newspaper the *Guardian* about Britain's pursuit of continental shelf extension claims and the 'new international politics of underwater prospecting' is captioned 'The New British Empire? UK Plans to Annex South Atlantic' (Bowcott, 2007). The message conveyed to readers, accurately or not, is that the United Kingdom is preparing territorial claims on thousands of square miles of the Atlantic Ocean[1] around the Falklands, Ascension Island and the island of Rockall, not just for the potentially lucrative oil, natural gas and minerals to be discovered along the continental slope, but equally as the next chapter in the Falklands war of the 1980s. The same can be said for what Klaus Dodds (2008) has called the 'icy geopolitics' of the Arctic.

In *The Deep*, a 2010 BBC science fiction series, noted English film actress Minnie Driver plays the captain of the *Orpheus*, a research submarine that descends into the vent fields of the Lomonosov Ridge[2] at the bottom of the Arctic Ocean in a quest to find a rare source of bio-fuels. Not only do the crew of the *Orpheus* face extreme danger from a Russian ghost ship with a damaged nuclear reactor, they inadvertently descend into a maelstrom of international intrigue involving unscrupulous oil companies, a rogue CIA agent and Russian–American geopolitical rivalries, clearly inspired by events following the Russian flag planting beneath the North Pole in 2007.

Popular action adventure series like *The Deep* cannot of course be confused with real life. Nevertheless, these fictional dramas often swim in the currents of contemporary geopolitics. For example, the initial segment of *Die Another Day* (2002), the twentieth film in the James Bond series, is set in North Korea. While negatively received on both sides of the Korean border (an official of the South Korean Ministry of Culture and Tourism called it 'the wrong film at the wrong time'), *Die Another Day* did bring images of a closed and brutal political regime to a mass audience, many of whom are likely to skip international news media coverage of foreign lands. Dodds (2007: 32–3) argues that the film's depiction of a crazed North Korean colonel plotting to eradicate South Korea and Japan with a powerful and destructive satellite coincided with US President George W. Bush's 'axis of evil' speech, thus contributing to the perception that the world was in the midst of great uncertainty and the Republican Party was better able than the Democrats to protect America from the threat of terrorism.

In the case of *The Deep*, the deadly plotting in the fictional Arctic 'International Maritime Exclusion Zone' may well be overdramatized, but as Dodds (2008: 1) warns, 'Given recent

Russian activity [in the Arctic Basin] and associated reactions from Arctic neighbours, it appears that some of the intrigue and tension that characterised the Cold War has returned.' Besides the Polar Regions, clashes have occurred in recent years between Britain and Argentina in the South Atlantic; France and Vanuatu in the Pacific; and China and its neighbours (Vietnam, Taiwan, the Philippines, Indonesia) in the South China Sea. Many of these situations are carryovers from longstanding boundary disputes that have been given new life by virtue of claims to an extended continental shelf outer limit that are being filed with the UN CLCS.

In his book *Maritime Power and the Law of the Sea* (2011), James Kraska argues that the public order of the oceans is being endangered by what he calls 'excessive claims in the EEZ'. These are of two main types. In the first instance, coastal states – Australia and Canada are said to be particular offenders – draw excessive baselines in order to push the EEZ further seawards to capture additional areas of the high seas. In the second case – China and Brazil are prime examples – coastal states draw a lawful baseline, but then assert sovereignty, jurisdiction or control over the EEZ to an extent that goes beyond what is permitted in the LOSC. Typically, this takes the form of passing domestic laws and regulations that restrict the right of foreign nations to conduct activities in the zone and then aggressively enforcing them militarily. Kraska (2011: 308) detects an unholy alliance of left-wing environmental activists and conservative sovereignty champions in Brazil, Canada, China and the United States that is dedicated to radically transforming the EEZ and promoting an agenda that 'destabilizes the liberal foundations of the order of the oceans'. Of course, Kraska is anything but a neutral observer. An American naval officer, attorney and adviser to the Joint Chiefs of Staff, he is dedicated to promoting a worldwide freedom of navigation policy that manifestly advantages US military security agencies and interests. The US Marine Corps, he believes, is 'the only armed force that focuses entirely on this central reality' (i.e. the erosion of the regime of the EEZ will probably be coupled with the breakdown of order ashore in coastal and inshore regions) (Kraska, 2011: 8). Nonetheless, Kraska's analysis does highlight the problem of 'creeping jurisdiction', which I noted in the previous chapter. More broadly, his account of the political economy of 'excessive' sovereignty and security claims over the EEZ points to the growing contest between the Governing the Abyss narrative and an opposing Sovereignty Games narrative.

Sovereignty Games

The term 'sovereignty game(s)' has been used by legal thinkers and political scientists since the late 1980s (Cleave, 1989; Zolberg, 1994). Most recently, the Danish scholars Rebecca Adler-Nissen and Thomas Gammeltoft-Hansen have edited a volume entitled *Sovereignty Games: Instrumentalizing State Sovereignty in Europe and Beyond* (2008a). The editors argue that national sovereignty is alive and well in the present age of globalization. Rather than turning their backs on it, states have become more instrumental, skilled and creative in their use of sovereignty to reassert legitimacy, power and control in the face of new regional and global challenges. Adler-Nissen and Gammeltoft-Hansen reject the notion, popular among some left-wing scholars, that sovereignty, and its henchman international law, are nothing more than a cover for imperialism, that is, tools deployed by First World countries to exploit Third World nations and their resources and to embed structural inequality in the international system.

The idea of 'games' is useful here, they tell their readers, as a way of underlining and bringing analytical attention to the dynamic nature of sovereignty. That is, sovereignty is more than just a fixed, formal legal and constitutional concept. Rather, it is something actually practised by real-life actors – individuals, state representatives and private companies on a day-to-day basis (Adler-Nissen and Gammeltoft-Hansen, 2008b: 203–4) and used in the context of treaty regimes such as the Antarctic Treaty (see below). Sovereignty games have three necessary components: rules, players and moves. It is important to keep in mind that the latter component, moves, has a strategic dimension – the skilled use of sovereignty claims, including anticipating likely reactions from others (Gammeltoft-Hansen and Adler-Nissen, 2008: 8).

To some extent, the Sovereignty Games narrative, as high-lighted in this chapter, continues to draw from classic 'West-phalian' or 'realist' power politics, which emphasizes the occupation and control of physical space and natural resources for the state, and the implications for international affairs, including military power and strategies for national security (Heininen, 2014: 244). Thus, some analysts of the contemporary politics of the Polar Regions (Arctic and Antarctic) are prone to channelling the notion of the 'Great Game' – strategic rivalries and conflicts that were played out in the nineteenth century between the British and Russian Empires, primarily in Central Asia.[3] In the contemporary context, this is variously labelled the 'new great game' (Fox, 2014); 'China's great game in the Arctic' (Giraudo, 2014); and the 'polar great game' (Hough, 2013). Nonetheless, sovereignty games as practised in the Arctic, and on the deep oceans, possess a discursive dimension that is missing from orthodox realist accounts.

Deep-Ocean Exploration, the Military and Security Politics

Exploration and investigation of the deep sea has been inter-twined with matters of national security, military strategy and political ambitions for quite a long time. Indeed, few of those involved in any type of marine research in the twentieth century were totally immune to this. Thus, in 1949, Eugenie Clark, the noted marine biologist and expert on sharks (see Acknowledgements), was sent by the US Navy to the South Seas to study poisonous fish (McFadden, 2015), presumably not just for reasons of scientific curiosity.

During World War II, a close relationship developed between oceanographers and the military in the United States. One consequence of this was the vast infusion of funds[4] and people into a field of marine research that had been struggling prior to the war. Indeed, as late as 1949, oceanography remained a little-known discipline. According to a committee of the National Academy of Sciences, at that date there were fewer than 100 oceanographers of all kinds in the United

States (Mills, 1983: 67). Additionally, the military engine shaped the form and content of oceanography:

> Perhaps the most important effect that the war had on the development of oceanography was the redistribution of interests within the field itself, and this was largely the result of the military's selection of research problems. For a period of three or four years it was the nature of the war, not the interests of the scientists, that determined which studies within oceanography would be pursued and which laid aside. (Schlee, 1973: 283)

As Jacob Darwin Hamblin documents in his book *Oceanographers and the Cold War* (2005), most oceanographic scientific work in the United States from 1945 onwards continued to be funded through defence expenditures. Oceanography, notes Hamblin (2005: xviii), was 'a Cold War science, tied to geopolitics as much as any other scientific field'. Among others, it dealt with aspects of undersea warfare such as submarine acoustics and sea-launched nuclear missiles. Hamblin (2005: xix) identifies a 'paradox' of oceanography after World War II: support for research was closely linked to national military projects, yet oceanography was 'an inherently individual endeavor'. He argues that the balance between nationalist and internationalist tendencies among American oceanographers was constantly shifting depending on the geopolitical context of the times. In the 1950s and early 1960s, there were numerous attempts to put cooperation into practice on a large scale: the International Geophysical Year (1957–8), the International Indian Ocean Expedition, the Scientific Committee on Oceanic Research and the Intergovernmental Oceanographic Commission. However, after the launch of *Sputnik* in 1957, many Western scientists felt increasingly disillusioned with cooperation and were more reluctant to promote international initiatives. Ironically, American oceanographers benefited from the anxiety sparked by the *Sputnik* launch, with Congressional support for marine research escalating dramatically, as did expenditures on space science and science education (Hamblin, 2005: 262).

One especially notable example of the close links between military patronage and deep-sea marine research during the

Cold War is the Heezen–Tharp mapping project. In 1957, two researchers at the Lamont Geological observatory, Bruce Heezen and Marie Tharp, published a physiographic map detailing 12 million square miles of sea floor in the North Atlantic Ocean. This was the first comprehensive map of any ocean basin, making it one of the most profound advances in mid-twentieth-century cartography. Furthermore, it provided crucial evidence in support of the theory of plate tectonics (Doel et al., 2006: 605–6).

Heezen had close professional connections with Bell Laboratories in Murray Hill, New Jersey, a major centre of military-industrial research in the 1950s. Ronald Doel and his co-authors (2006) note that this connection was of enormous help, for several reasons. First, Heezen supplemented his military contracts at Lamont with contracts from Bell Labs. Second, the researchers gained access to sea-floor data well beyond those otherwise available. In the early 1950s, Bell Labs was active in a number of projects involving underwater telecommunications cables. Partly this was a reflection of its attempts to devise new methods of repairing cable breaks (telegraph cable breaks were common owing to corrosion). However, Bell was also pursuing a project, code-named TAT-1, that planned to lay cables for the first undersea telephone line from the United States to Britain. A parallel (and secret) project involved laying cables for the SOSUS undersea submarine surveillance system using similar materials. Accurate maps were absolutely crucial to this.

In a similar key, Naomi Oreskes (2003) demonstrates that the Cold War context was highly productive of advances in oceanographic research, inasmuch as patronage from the US Office of Naval Research (ONR)[5] provided substantial funding to scientists for projects that required the use of deep submergence research vehicles. She focuses specifically on the US Navy's interest in the deep sea, which led to the discovery of hydrothermal vents on the sea floor. The vent discoveries were made possible by a novel technology designed to allow humans to explore and work in ocean environments. Rather than being motivated by pure scientific curiosity, the Navy's interest here was rooted in the political concerns of the Cold War, and specifically in its desire to monitor the movements of Soviet submarines and be prepared for deep-sea rescue and salvage of its own craft (Oreskes, 2003: 700) (see Box 3.1).

As Oreskes tells it, throughout the 1950s, as global political tensions mounted, the Navy became fixated on developing underwater acoustics systems designed to detect and track Soviet submarines. A decade later, spurred by the *Thresher* disaster, this shifted to a concern with deep search, salvage and rescue. The *Thresher* was a US fast-attack submarine that was lost at sea with all hands killed on 10 April 1963 while undertaking a test dive off the coast of Cape Cod. Using all available means of detection – underwater photography,

---

Box 3.1 Raising the *Red Star*

One of the more unsavoury examples of military activity being carried out under the pretext of deep-sea exploration and discovery took place in the early 1970s. In the summer of 1974, Summa Corporation, owned and controlled by the reclusive American billionaire Howard Hughes, launched the *Glomar Explorer* (not to be confused with the *Glomar Challenger*), a massive ship built by Global Marine. The stated purpose of the *Glomar Explorer*'s voyage was the commercial recovery of manganese nodules from the sea floor. In reality, its real aim of Project Jennifer (its CIA code name) was to raise the *Red Star*, a nuclear-armed Soviet submarine that had gone down in the North Pacific 750 miles northwest of Hawaii. As it happened, the salvage operation was bungled, with the badly damaged submarine falling apart more than a mile from its resting place. David Helvarg (2006: 17–20) reports that Project Jennifer provoked an unexpected outcome. To lend credibility to its cover story, the CIA placed dozens of enthusiastic articles about the prospects for mining the vast mineral wealth on the ocean floor in scientific journals and major periodicals such as *Business Week*, the *New York Times* and the *Wall Street Journal*. This publicity contributed significantly to invigorating the commercial race to mine the oceans. It prompted the formation of several consortia[6] in the early 1970s dedicated to deep-sea manganese nodule mining. More significantly, it sparked a political backlash against manganese nodule mining at the ongoing UNCLOS III talks in Caracas, Venezuela (see Chapter 2).

echo-sounding, magnetometry, radiation – it took more than a year to locate the wreckage of the *Thresher*. As a result, support grew for the establishment of a permanent Navy Office in Deep Submergence whose primary goal should be the development of a small manned submersible capable of rescuing crews trapped in a disabled submarine (Oreskes, 2003: 711).

Much of the remainder of Oreskes' article is devoted to tracing the history of *Alvin*, the first and most durable submersible vessel capable of exploring the deep sea. Funded by the ONR and operated by the Woods Hole Oceanographic Institution, *Alvin* rotated between scientific work and Navy missions, with the latter taking precedence. In the winter of 1966, for instance, *Alvin* participated in the heavily publicized recovery of an unarmed hydrogen bomb that had plunged into the Mediterranean Sea near the Spanish coastal village of Palomares. Nonetheless, *Alvin* also played a crucial role in a major scientific discovery. In 1977, a scientific team led by Robert Ballard and Jack Corliss observed and photographed for the first time active hydrothermal springs (vents) surrounded by complex biotic communities thriving under conditions previously thought inimical to life.

In the conclusion to her article, Oreskes points out that military projects like the *Thresher* search and the Palomares hydrogen bomb recovery, and pure scientific problems such as hydrothermal vent ecology, are extremes. Most of the applied scientific projects pursued by oceanographers during this period 'were questions that came into focus through the crosshairs of national security' (Oreskes, 2003: 730). That is, they pursued scientific topics about the natural world that interested them, but these interests emerged against the landscape of the Cold War, were shaped by the realities of military patronage and funding and remained dominant even after the political context that had inspired them changed.

During the Cold War, this conjunction of the military and the scientific was especially pertinent in the Polar North and under the deep seas. Both the United States and the Soviet Union were determined to make the seabed of the Arctic Ocean 'legible' for geopolitical reasons (Dodds, 2010a: 65). There were two fundamental motivations for this. In peaceful times, the priority was tracking and monitoring enemy naval submarines. Especially with the introduction of the Polaris nuclear submarines, tracking enemy submarines under the Arctic ice (and across the North Atlantic and North Pacific) became a high Navy priority (Coffey, 2002: 346). In the event of a crisis, superior oceanographic knowledge would provide a decisive military benefit. This was not just a matter of surveillance. The more naval forces understood about the hidden world of the Arctic Basin – its topography, salinity, icebergs, water temperatures, sea storms – the greater their strategic and operational advantage.

'Taking the Ocean's Temperature with Sound'

The close relationship between the military and the major oceanographic research institutions that was nurtured during the Cold War has carried over to more recent times. In the 1990s, a controversy arose over an experiment that was designed to search for signs of global climate change by 'taking the ocean's temperature with sound' (Hlebica, 2002: 25). The Acoustic Thermometry of Ocean Climate (ATOC) project was undertaken by scientists from the Scripps Institution of Oceanography and a university partner, funded by a $35 million contract awarded by the Defense Advanced Research Projects Agency (DARPA). Evidently, the partnership came about as a result of an initiative from Al Gore, then a senator from Tennessee, who encouraged the military to use its equipment and knowledge to advance understanding of environmental change (Siegel, 1999). The main principle behind the ATOC project is that sound travels more quickly in warmer water. The researchers therefore proposed transmitting long bursts of loud, low-frequency sound from transmitters built about half a mile down through the Pacific Ocean from California to New Zealand. Data was to be monitored at 13 listening posts around the Pacific, many of them run by the US Navy (Pearce, 1994).

The ATOC project provoked sharp opposition, both at acrimonious public hearings and as an electronic protest campaign spearheaded by segments of the marine biology community. The latter was conducted over a marine science bulletin board on the Internet and led to questions being raised in the US Congress (Pearce, 1994). Opponents worried that the transmission of sound waves throughout entire ocean basins would harm marine life, possibly leading to the gradual deafening and extinction of humpback whales. In the final segment of her three-part special series on CNN.com, Stephanie Siegel (1999) raised some troubling possibilities. One likely outcome of the ATOC project, as well as other low-frequency active sonars (LFASs), was the establishment of more extensive and sophisticated technologies for detecting submarines at long distances. In addition to the United States, Japan and Russia have been active in this area of applied science. Environmentalists fear that in the future a grid of near-continuous sound will be produced to map the world's oceans and everything in them, a scenario rejected by the ONR as 'science fiction' (Siegel, 1999).

International Geophysical Year 1957–8

This confluence of security and science was especially visible during the International Geophysical Year (IGY), which ran from 1 July 1957 to 31 December 1958. The idea for the IGY originated in 1950 during a Washington area dinner party at the home of prominent American space scientist James Van Allen (after whom the Van Allen radiation belt is named), where a suggestion for holding a third 'Polar Year' (the first two of these were held in 1882–3 and 1932–3) morphed into a broader proposal to pursue physical knowledge of the entire planet and its upper atmosphere. The IGY attracted participation from nearly 70 countries over 11 fields of study. Seventy ships from 35 nations participated in the marine investigations (Schlee, 1973: 346). It has been called 'the largest and most ambitious scientific collaboration the world had ever seen' (Good, 2010: 177). And, without a doubt, the IGY was a windfall for oceanographers. This was especially true in the United States: the ocean sciences component ($2,035,791) was a small part of the total of IGY funding, but nonetheless it surpassed any previous support for ocean research in the research division of the National Science Foundation (Jennings, 2000).

An explicit policy of never discussing politics was to be its 'guiding light'. Even the descriptor 'international' was meant to distinguish it from 'intergovernmental' pursuits. IGY planners deliberately excluded the discipline of geology from the list of official IGY sciences to be studied in Antarctica. Geology, they argued, 'was thought to be too political: someone might discover a valuable mineral resource, which could set off a "gold rush" and inflame adversarial relationships or the claims issue' (Belanger, 2010: 268). Nevertheless, many geologists participated in IGY projects, especially in the Antarctic. But, right from the beginning, the IGY was heavily 'laden with politics'. This was, after all, the era of the Cold War, during which science, exploration and geopolitics were perceived by many political leaders and journalists to be 'a dangerous if necessary cocktail which had to be handled carefully' (Dodds, 2010b: 160). Increasing Soviet participation in the IGY created profound geopolitical unease, centred in particular on the Antarctic, where the Soviet Union had recently become active again (Hamblin, 2005: 62–3). Furthermore, the 1957 withdrawal from the IGY of the People's Republic of China – it objected to the last-minute inclusion of Taiwan in the scientific programme[7] – undercut the idea that the IGY was capable of transcending political differences.

Western scientists and governments never trusted Soviet oceanographers. The former thought Russian scientists were backward, while the latter suspected them of doing work of a military nature. The launch of *Sputnik* – which in fact was an announced part of their planned scientific programme – dispelled notions that the Soviets were technologically inferior, but it posed a direct challenge to the technological supremacy of the United States. The launch, Hamblin (2005: 91) claims, 'did the most to shatter the spirit of the IGY'.

For their part, the Americans and Canadians were scarcely immune from undertaking projects and activities with a military purpose. In August 1958, for example, the nuclear-powered submarine USS *Nautilus* sailed under the North Pole, as did its sister vessel the USS *Skate* six months later.[8] These voyages undoubtedly provided greater scientific understanding of the Arctic Ocean Basin, even as they gave fresh impetus to the ONR (Dodds, 2010a: 65).

Contemporary Conflicts

The South China Sea

The *Quadrennial Defense Review* is a Congressionally mandated review of the US Department of Defense strategy and priorities that is made available to the public on the Internet. In its 2014 *Review*, the Pentagon prioritizes the Asia Pacific region, and especially China:

> The Asia Pacific region is increasingly central to global commerce, politics and security. Defense spending in this region continues to rise. As nations in the region continue to develop their military and security capabilities, there is greater risk that tensions over long-standing sovereignty disputes or claims to natural resources will spur disruptive competition or erupt into conflict, reversing the trends of rising regional peace, stability and prosperity. In particular, the rapid pace and comprehensive scope of China's military modernization continues, combined with a relative lack of transparency and openness from China's leaders regarding both military capabilities and intentions. (US Department of Defense, 2014: 1–4)

While the authors do not go into specifics, some of the 'tensions' cited in the *Quadrennial Defense Review* 2014 apply to military and non-military (scarce resources, ecosystem changes, global warming) security concerns (see also Jacques, 2003: 67–102).

One perennial flashpoint is the South China Sea,[9] a body of water containing more than 200 small islands, rocks and reefs. The South China Sea has more overlapping claims than anywhere else in the world (McLean and Readel, 2007: 206). Sources of conflict here include historical disagreements on sovereignty, energy clashes, threats to maritime security and overlapping claims related to UNCLOS. Disputants include China, Vietnam, the Philippines, Malaysia, Indonesia, Brunei and Taiwan, with other 'extra-regional' countries (India, Japan, Russia and the United States) guarding their own interests in the region closely. A particular source of conflicting sovereignty claims are the Spratly and Paracel Islands (which China calls the Xisha Islands).

A chief point of contention in the South China Sea has been what is called the 'U-shaped line' or 'nine-dash line'. This is a line with nine segments off the Chinese coast that has been displayed on all Chinese maps of the region since 1948, as well as in government documents, and even in Air China's in-flight magazine (Perlez, 2012). Michael Sheng-ti Gau (2014) notes that the U-shaped line was not visible on an earlier map published in 1935 by the Republic of China, but each of the maritime features on the 1948 map could be identified on an accompanying list. Nonetheless, concludes Gau (2014: 104), 'If compared with the 1945 Truman Proclamation [see Chapter 2 of this book] and the contemporary maritime zonal declarations by other states, the 1948 Chinese map obviously fell short of an average or proper maritime zonal claim.' Its official Chinese name is 'traditional maritime boundary line' (*chuantong haijiang xian*). As Zou Keyuan (2012a: 18–19) points out, 'It is unknown whether what China claims within the line is its national territory, including the islands, underwater rocks, the seabed and the water column.' What *is* certain is that China's neighbours, notably Malaysia, the Philippines, Taiwan and Vietnam, categorically reject the legitimacy of the U-shaped line, regarding China's claim as 'exaggerated and legally groundless', as one Vietnamese official put it (Keyuan, 2012b: 174).

Indonesia and the Philippines have gone so far as to submit diplomatic notes at the United Nations stating that the 'nine-dash line' has no legal basis in international law. On 23 January 2013, the Philippines took this a step further, presenting a diplomatic notification to China that it was preparing to initiate arbitration proceedings as set out under Article 287 and Annex VII of the LOSC in order to challenge China's claims and entitlement to areas of the South China Sea and the underlying seabed. While some legal commentators (e.g. Gau, 2014) have expressed reservations about whether the Philippines' claims are well founded in fact and law, nevertheless this signifies that sovereignty clashes in the South China Sea are escalating.

For its part, the Chinese government has ramped up both its rhetoric and its actions. On 31 July 2012, the 85th anniversary of the founding of the People's Liberation Army, the Chinese Defence Ministry announced 'a regular combat-readiness patrol system' which was designed to maintain 'marine sovereignty' in the waters in the sea under China's jurisdiction. Around the same time, China established a larger army garrison and expanded the size of a putative legislature on Yongxing, a tiny island in the Paracel/Xisha Islands, claimed by both China and Vietnam (Perlez, 2012).

Earlier that year, there was a months-long standoff between lightly armed vessels belonging to the Philippines and China at the Scarborough Shoal, a triangular-shaped island group off the coast of the Philippines, 550 miles from Hainan Island, the closest Chinese port. The incident was sparked by allegations that the Chinese were fishing illegally in the area, as well as taking away ecologically sensitive corals. Soon after, the USS *North Carolina*, a first-attack submarine, surfaced unexpectedly in Subic Bay, in the economic free port zone of the Philippines province of Zambales. Security analysts considered this significant because the United States and the Philippines had previously been moving apart, with the former shifting its naval bases to Guam. Writing for the *Huffington Post*, global risk analyst Daniel Wagner and his co-authors (2012) observed, 'The rising tension over the Scarborough Shoal has served to raise the Philippines' profile once again, both as a potential adversary of China and as a reliable ally of the US.'

Some of the sharpest clashes have occurred between China and Vietnam since 2009. These seem to have been prompted, in part, by Vietnam's claims to the UN CLCS. The incidents here (see Amer, 2014: 20–3) are reminiscent of the 'gunboat diplomacy' that characterized international politics in earlier times: Chinese patrol forces arrested three Vietnamese fishing boats that were said to be violating a 'fishing ban' (June 2009), spurring months of Vietnamese protests; a Chinese maritime surveillance vessel allegedly cut the exploration cables of a seismic vessel of the Viet Nam National Oil and Gas Group while it was conducting a seismic survey on the continental shelf of Vietnam (May 2011); Chinese fishing boats and a Vietnamese seismic ship collided, with the exploration cables of the latter being slashed, a result variously of the fishing boats deliberately ramming the oil and gas vessel (the Vietnamese version), or the fishing nets of the former getting tangled with the cables of the ship during an illegal chase initiated by 'armed Vietnamese ships' (the Chinese version) (June 2011).

Another source of controversy that has played out in the South China Sea is the question of whether the conduct of military activities in the EEZ of another country is legitimate. This is a grey area under international maritime law. The LOSC does not mention military use, only freedoms such as navigation, overflight and the laying of submarine cables and pipelines. In common with other coastal states such as Brazil, India and Pakistan, China restricts unapproved military exercises or activities in or over its EEZs, including hydrographic surveying and intelligence collection (Keyuan, 2012b: 171–2).

In 2001 there was an incident where the USNS *Bowditch*, an American oceanographic survey ship, entered China's EEZ in the Yellow Sea, was confronted by a Chinese frigate and ordered to leave. *Bowditch* changed course and left the area, as instructed. After filing a protest with the Chinese Ministry of Foreign Affairs, however, the United States sent *Bowditch* back into the area, this time with an armed escort (Keyuan, 2012b; Pedrozo, 2009).

Eight years later, a similar incident occurred in China's claimed EEZ approximately 75 miles south of Hainan Island in the South China Sea. Five Chinese vessels – a Navy intelligence ship, a government fisheries patrol vessel, a state oceanographic patrol vessel and two small fishing trawlers – surrounded the military survey ship. Citing Sam Bateman's (2009) analysis, James Kraska (2011) points out that the official classification of a 'sovereign immune' naval vessel is more than just a matter of semantics. In its role as an oceanographic survey ship, USNS *Bowditch* is officially part of marine scientific research, which is under the jurisdiction of a coastal state in its EEZ (see Chapter 2). By contrast, USNS *Impeccable* is classified as a US naval ocean surveillance ship, making its presence in Chinese EEZ waters more legally permissible, in that military uses of the seas are recognized by international law (Kraska, 2011: 252–3). A near collision – Kraska (2011: 252) calls it 'a shoving match' – ensued between the trawlers and the American ship. As in the 2001 incident, the US government protested to the Chinese, who replied that the *Impeccable*'s presence in China's claimed EEZ violated international law. The *Impeccable* returned to the area the next day, under escort of a guided-missile destroyer, the USS *Chung-Hoon* (Pedrozo, 2009).

Kraska (2011: 322–3) describes both the *Bowditch* and *Impeccable* incidents as 'manufactured'. The Chinese, he says, had three strategic goals in mind. First, this was designed to strengthen China's hand in the contest with its neighbours to dominate the East China Sea, South China Sea and Yellow Sea by de-legitimizing the presence in the region of the US Navy and allied naval forces. It was likely no accident that one week before the *Impeccable* incident, Li Guao'an, a member of the Chinese People's Political Consultative Conference, urged China to take greater steps to protect its 'blue territory'. Second, in both cases the confrontation occurred around the time a new US President assumed office – George W. Bush in 2001 and Barack Obama in 2009 – providing the Chinese with a good opportunity to test the incoming administration. Finally, there was a potential domestic payoff. As Kraska (2011: 322) explains,

> By manufacturing an incident, the Beijing government could feed a political narrative inside China of resisting the West, a message that strengthens the legitimacy of the Communist Party. The Chinese tactic leverages a number of powerful storylines, including fanning Chinese nationalism and a sense of historical humiliation and injustice inflicted by the West, all packed in an unorthodox but effective (mis)interpretation of the EEZ that mixes terms of art and legal regimes contained in UNCLOS.

Incidents such as this have prompted the United States to step up the pace of research into 'cheap stealth' technologies that can be sequestered without detection on the ocean floor (see Box 3.2). While the US military has undertaken these cheap stealth programmes as a cost-effective alternative to manned submarines and submersibles, there is another purpose that is directly linked to changing global geopolitics. As the excerpt from the 2014 *Quadrennial Defense Review* (above) suggests, the Obama administration has become very concerned with China's rising influence and threats to sea-lanes used by other nations in the Pacific Ocean. However, it has become increasingly difficult to use conventional ships and aircraft for surveillance purposes in this region because the Chinese are deploying long-range missiles and other defence systems (in military jargon these are known as 'anti-access, area-denial weapons'). To get around this, the Pentagon has called for more technology such as the robot probes of the UFP programme (see Box 3.2) that will enable it to place assets closer to potential targets on the Chinese mainland without attracting attention (Locker, 2014).

Kraska (2011: 279) comments, 'The last decade has seen technological breakthroughs in machine robotics, nanotechnology, and autonomous marine devices that portend a future in which distant maritime states operate numerous unmanned surface and underwater systems in the EEZ of coastal states.' The legal status of these devices is not entirely clear. Evidently, this issue arose during the UNCLOS III negotiations, with the Group of 77 arguing that their construction, maintenance, deployment and operation should be banned, a provision strongly opposed by the major maritime states. Ultimately, a compromise was reached which gave coastal states jurisdiction over installations and structures for resource, environmental and marine science purposes, but said nothing about the emplacement of foreign military installations and structures on or under the seabed of the EEZ or the continental shelf. Other treaty law, notably that pertaining to maritime safety and to toxic dumping, has suggested that unmanned vehicles may be characterized as 'watercraft, notably, ships or submarines', but this does not take into account the 'variation between manned systems and unmanned systems such as size of the means of propulsion, type of platform, capability, endurance, human versus autonomous control, and mission set' (Kraska, 2011: 284).

There is of course another way of looking at this. Peter Nolan (2013) argues that the pattern of 'bullying behaviour' exhibited by China in the region pales in comparison with the aggressive exploitation of maritime claims in the EEZ adjacent to their territorial sea by the United States and the European Union states. This 'colossal resource grab' by former colonial powers 'has almost entirely escaped international attention' (Nolan, 2013: 78). Nolan maintains that the provision in the LOSC that permits islands to establish the

Box 3.2 Cheap Stealth

More than half-a-century after the historic dives of the *Nautilus* and *Skate*, the US military continues to engage in science and surveillance activities in remote corners of the deep ocean. Rather than rely on ships and submarines, however, the Navy is experimenting with the use of 'cheap stealth', that is, self-powered robotic military systems. In part, at least, these new technologies are a response to cuts in US military spending.

One example of this is the 'Upward Falling Payloads' (UFP) programme being run by DARPA. These are deployable robot pods or nodes that hibernate in special containers on the deep-sea floor for years at a time. When needed, they can be activated remotely by a secret signal and sent to the surface. Not weapons per se, they are equipped to provide 'a range of non-lethal but useful capabilities such as situational awareness, disruption, deception, networking, rescue, or any other mission that benefits from being pre-distributed and hidden' (*Homeland Security News Wire*, 2013a). DARPA has indicated that the UFP programme, if it is found to be technologically feasible and affordable, will be targeted for the almost half of global waters that are more than 4 kilometres deep (Locker, 2014).

In another 'cheap stealth' project, the ONR and the US Naval Undersea Warfare Center have funded a multi-university[10] nationwide $5 million project, the goal of which is to build large robotic jellyfish to patrol the oceans. The size and weight of a grown man, these robotic jellyfish are powered by rechargeable nickel metal hydride batteries and are designed to operate on their own for months (*Homeland Security News Wire*, 2013b). While they could be used to study schools of fish, monitor ocean currents or clean up oil spills, they are also likely to play a role in covert military surveillance operations (Angley, 2013). Like *Alvin*, the pioneering submersible vessel that operated in the 1960s and 1970s, presumably military missions would trump the environmental and scientific ones. While robots modelled after aquatic creatures (eels have also been considered) are seen to be cost effective, they also appeal to the military because they are more difficult to identify than are the drones and tethered vehicles presently used by the Navy to detect mines and map the ocean floor (McConnaughey, 2012).

same EEZ of 200 nautical miles as nation states is a huge loophole that has been exploited by former imperial powers that have maintained control over a scattering of far-flung territories. Thus, China has only around 347,000 square miles of undisputed EEZ adjacent to the mainland, plus a further area, probably less than 772,000 square miles, claimed in the South China Sea; by contrast, the United States has 3.7 million square miles of EEZ in the Pacific Ocean alone.

The Indian Ocean

Until the mid-1990s, India was the dominant power in the Indian Ocean; other potential players in the power politics of the region – Indonesia, Australia, Pakistan, Iran and South Africa – were minimally involved (Jayewardene, 2001: 124). Additionally, the global superpowers, especially the United States and the Soviet Union, maintained a presence in the region, a carryover from the late 1960s and early 1970s, when they deployed long-range missile systems and nuclear submarines during the Cold War.

With the implementation of the LOSC agreement, the geopolitics of the Indian Ocean began to shift. Both India and Pakistan asserted their right to restrict foreign military activities in their EEZ and on the continental shelf without obtaining the consent of other powers. Furthermore, India claimed the right under the LOSC to construct, maintain and operate artificial islands, offshore terminals and other structures deemed necessary for resource exploration and exploitation and/or the convenience of shipping (Kraska, 2011: 310).

Significantly, a new political player, China, entered onto the scene. In November 2011, COMRA signed a 15-year contract with the ISA through which it obtained exclusive rights to prospect and explore for polymetallic sulphides in 10,000 square kilometres of seabed in the southwest Indian Ocean in an area off the coast of Africa. While this is beyond its national maritime jurisdiction, nevertheless, there appears to be considerable unease in Indian security circles. Maritime Security.Asia, an online news service, reported that the Directorate of Naval Intelligence (DNI) 'had expressed concern that COMRA's access could have strategic implications for

India's security' (*MaritimeSecurity.Asia*, 2011), while the Indian Defence Forum (2011), an Internet blog, stated that DNI had informed the Indian government that 'the contract would provide an excuse for China to operate its warships, besides compiling data on the vast mineral resources in India's backyard.' It remains to be seen whether there is real reason for concern here or whether this is a kind of security fantasy.[11]

The Polar Regions

Arctic Dreams

In August 2014, just as he had every year since coming to office in 2006, Canadian Prime Minister Stephen Harper, together with an entourage of staffers, senior cabinet ministers and journalists, travelled to the high Arctic for his summer tour. Harper's 'northern mission' was clearly politically directed. Geopolitically, it was designed to reinforce Canada's presence in the Arctic, where Canada and Russia have colliding interests, based on claims to the Lomonosov Ridge[12] between Ellesmere Island and Siberia, and what are believed to be vast oil and gas resources (Den Tandt, 2014). Domestically, Harper's vision of northern sovereignty was meant to shore up support for a government that had been lagging badly in opinion polls and was facing a national election in the near future. In 2013, in another piece of 'icy geopolitics', Citizenship and Immigration Minister Chris Alexander reached deep into his rhetorical kit bag by issuing Santa Claus with Canadian citizenship (Hopper, 2014; Paris, 2013).

In 2014, Harper hit the jackpot. In early September, he jubilantly announced that a lost ship, HMS *Erebus*, from the legendary Franklin expedition (named after its commander, British Rear Admiral Sir John Franklin) had been located by a Canadian team. Marine archaeologists had been searching with little luck for the *Erebus* for 170 years, after the vessel set out in 1845 in search of the Northwest Passage, the much sought-after link between the Atlantic and Pacific oceans, and became trapped in Arctic ice. Harper's Conservative government made the quest to discover what had become of the

Franklin expedition a priority in 2008, committing millions of dollars to the venture.

The search for and discovery of HMS *Erebus* is a prime example of how 'sovereignty games' in the Arctic are firmly embedded in a discursive context. Packaged by the media as 'one of history's biggest mysteries', the Franklin expedition has long been the subject of numerous songs, poems and novels. An Associated Press story published soon after Harper's announcement illustrates a narrative thread that has typically characterized both the search for the lost ship and its geopolitical significance: 'Harper's government made the project a priority as it looked to assert Canada's sovereignty over the Northwest Passage, where melting Arctic ice in recent years has unlocked the very shipping route Franklin was after' (Gillies, 2014). In this context, the Franklin project can be seen as being another weapon in an arsenal of 'effective occupation' of the Arctic (Dittmer et al., 2011: 8) that includes a promised polar icebreaker, a deep-water port at Nanisivik in Nunavut, an Arctic Research Station at Cambridge Bay and the 'Canadian (Inuit) Rangers', a somewhat ragtag Canadian Forces team who are tasked with engaging in surveillance and sovereignty patrols as Canada's first line of defence in the far North.

Canada is not alone in asserting its sovereign presence in the Arctic. In the autumn of 2013, Russia announced plans to resume a permanent Arctic military presence, beginning with rebuilding old Soviet-era bases across its Arctic territory, including in the Novosibirsk Archipelago (New Siberian Islands) (Den Tandt, 2014). Six years earlier, on an Arctic expedition to collect oceanographic and geophysical data in support of its application to the UN CLCS, oceanographer Artur Chilingarov[13] famously planted a titanium Russian flag at the bottom of the Arctic Ocean, beaming televised pictures to the world.

In 2012, Artur Chilingarov told journalist Matthew Fisher, 'The most active country in the Arctic right now is China.' As well as building a fleet of icebreakers and ice-strengthened cargo ships, he noted, the Chinese are learning how to drill far deeper in the ocean than any other country (Fisher, 2012a). In September 2014, the *New York Times* printed a story about rising alarm in Norway over the imminent sale of a huge tract of Arctic land two and a half times bigger than Manhattan to Chinese business tycoon Huang Nubo, who is thought by some to be a straw man for the Chinese Communist Party. Ownership of the land parcels, a waterfront plot near the northern mainland city of Tromsø and a property on Spitsbergen, the main island in the Svalbard archipelago,[14] would put China just within the Arctic Circle. As part of the *Times* piece, Andrew Higgins interviewed Willy Ostreng, the President of the Norwegian Scientific Academy for Polar Research. Ostreng cited a list of recent Chinese actions in the Polar North: investing in an icebreaker, *The Snow Dragon*; sending scientists to Svalbard to join teams of international researchers; successfully lobbying to become an observer at the Arctic Council; and seeking (unsuccessfully) to build a large radar antenna on Svalbard. 'For anyone interested in geopolitics, this is the region to follow in years to come', Ostreng concluded, and 'the perception is that China wants a foothold in the Arctic' (Higgins, 2014).

These days much of the conversation over sovereignty in the Arctic revolves around claims submitted to a United Nations body established by the LOSC, the CLCS. This is made possible by a provision under Article 76 of the LOSC that allows that a coastal state might be able to assert subsurface rights over that part of the continental shelf that extends beyond the existing 200-nautical-mile limit pertaining to the EEZ provided that the country can prove that a geographical link exists between its land mass and adjacent underwater formations. There are two formulae that coastal states can use to determine this: the Gardiner Line and the Hedberg Line.[15] As one might expect, this is an extremely complex, detailed and costly process that depends on detailed geo-scientific assessments. It is also one with high stakes: the US Geological Survey estimates that the Arctic holds about 13% of the world's undiscovered conventional oil and 20% of its undiscovered natural gas resources (Koranyi, 2012).

Denmark is the first nation past the post, officially laying a comprehensive claim to the North Pole and any potential energy resources beneath it before the CLCS in December 2014. Bolstered by CDN $64 million in Arctic scientific research, the Danes claimed 895,000 square kilometres, including thousands of hectares of the sea floor previously claimed by Russia. The basis of the Danish claim is the assertion that the Lomonosov Ridge is actually an extension of Greenland (Hopper, 2014).

Klaus Dodds (2010c) characterizes the political geographies of the outer continental shelf in the Arctic as an uneasy mix of cooperation and competition. On the one hand, Arctic coastal states seek certainty and recognition since stability is necessary for orderly commercial development. Even the United States, which has yet to sign on the LOSC but is nonetheless a stakeholder by virtue of its territories in the Gulf of Alaska, the Arctic Ocean and the Bering Sea, recognizes this. This is evidenced by its investment in the Extended Continental Shelf Project (ECSP), whose mission it is to establish the full extent of the continental shelf in the United States consistent with international law.

On the other hand, political gamesmanship will not shrivel away any time soon. For example, five coastal states in the Arctic (Dodds labels these the 'Arctic Five' or 'A5') – Canada, Denmark, Norway, Russia and the United States – acted collectively to sign the 2008 'Illulissat Declaration' asserting that they are willing to be guided by the LOSC as a mechanism to resolve any overlapping claims. This seems quite reasonable, but it explicitly excludes other members (Finland, Iceland, Sweden) of the Arctic Council, a regional body established in the 1990s, as well as indigenous communities in the North such as the Inuit. The bottom line, then, is that some Arctic players risk ending up more equal than others.

While it is evident that the key political players in the Arctic region are engaging in considerable geopolitical posturing, along with a bit of sabre-rattling, it is not yet clear whether this will trigger any actual incidents of the type that have been occurring in the South China Sea. Gwynne Dyer (2012), a Canadian journalist and military historian who comments frequently in the media on security issues, thinks this is unlikely. The race for Arctic resources, Dyer ventures, is 'mostly rhetoric'. There are, he says, three separate 'resources' in the Arctic. On the surface ocean are sea-lanes that are opening up to commercial traffic along the northern coasts of Russia and Canada as the sea ice recedes. Testifying in May 2012 before the US Senate, then Secretary of State Hillary Clinton prioritized these routes, 'It is more important that we put our navigational rights on a treaty footing and have a larger voice in the interpretation and development of the rules. You will soon see China, India, Brazil, you name it – all vying for navigational rights and routes through the Arctic' (Koranyi, 2012).

There are two additional types of resources: potential oil and gas deposits that can be drilled once the ice retreats; and the water itself between the seabed and the surface, what Dyer (2012) calls 'the planet's last unfinished ocean', which is economically important primarily as a fishing ground. While some disagreements may arise, notably over hydrocarbon deposits under the Arctic seabed, Dyer doubts that any of these will actually lead to armed conflict. In a 2012 interview, Victor Posyolov, head of Russia's Arctic programme, told Matthew Fisher that he foresaw little possibility of conflict over the issue of overlapping claims for the Arctic in the near future. Russia and Canada, he forecast, would be likely to split the Lomonosov Ridge at or near its middle. It was far more likely, Posyolov predicted, that Canada and Denmark would have a difference of opinion over the ridge where it runs closest to Greenland and Canada's Ellesmere Island. In any case, it would probably take several decades for the pending Arctic claims to be sorted out, precluding any modern-day gold rush to stake claims in the Far North (Fisher, 2012b).

Nonetheless, the polar states (A8) remain unsettled. When Swedish naval forces recently sighted a suspicious underwater object in the waters off Stockholm, preceded by a distress call on a frequency used by the Russians, the Swedes launched a massive search operation involving up to 300 men, several stealth ships, minesweepers and helicopters (Coughlin, 2014). This has also led to a state of near hysteria in the Swedish media. One newspaper printed a photo of a 'suspicious' man in black in the search area, only to discover that he was only a Stockholm pensioner out fishing for trout (Morris, 2014). Rear Admiral Anders Grenstad, deputy chief of operations in the search, told the BBC that, if a submarine was discovered, weapons could be used to make it surface (*BBC News*, 2014). No doubt this serves as a reminder of the 1970s and 1980s and reflects the current unstable geopolitical situation in which the Baltic nations are wary of Russian intentions in the wake of Putin's military intervention in Crimea and Ukraine.

Antarctic Hopes

When we last visited the Antarctic in this chapter, it was during the International Geophysical Year (1957–8). As you might remember, the Soviet Union had once again started to express an interest in the region, a geopolitical development that left the Western powers uneasy. A year after the IGY ended (1959), a landmark agreement, the Antarctic Treaty, was signed, coming into force in 1961. Initially there were a dozen signatories. Seven of these – Argentina, Australia, Chile, France, New Zealand, Norway and the United Kingdom – are known as 'claimant states', meaning that they had asserted sovereignty claims over sectors of the Antarctic Peninsula based on either prior exploration and discovery or geographical contiguity. Another five nations – Belgium, Japan, South Africa, Russia and the United States – have not made or, in the case of Japan, cannot legally make claims. Today there are 47 parties to the Antarctic Treaty.

Dodds declares that the Antarctic Treaty transformed the legal, political and scientific status of the continent and the surrounding Southern Ocean. It is routinely described, he notes, 'as being the cornerstone of a system of governance alongside a host of other legal instruments and institutions that shape the governance of Antarctica' (Dodds, 2010c: 108). It might be helpful at this point to clarify what the Antarctic Treaty and its governing system, the Antarctic Treaty System (ATS), is and is not.

Essentially, the Antarctic Treaty was an attempt to create a nuclear-free zone at the bottom of the world. It declared that 'in the interests of all [hu]mankind' – note the parallel to the 'common heritage of [hu]mankind' principle[16] employed by Arvid Pardo and the LOSC – Antarctica is to be 'a natural reserve devoted to peace and science'. Both nuclear weapons and the disposal of radioactive materials are prohibited. The Treaty also exists to encourage the free exchange of scientific information.

What the Antarctic Treaty has not addressed are sovereignty claims. By signing, a nation neither endorses nor revokes the legal status that existed prior to the Treaty, nor does it acknowledge the validity of the seven existing territorial claims (Dodds, 2010c: 109). Two of the original signatories – the United States and the Soviet Union (Russia) – are classified as 'semi-claimants', by which is meant they reserve the right to make a claim in the future.

That future may well involve oil and gas as well as mineral resources, if these can possibly be extracted more easily as a result of Antarctic glaciers melting. To do so, however, would contravene the Protocol on Environmental Protection (Madrid Protocol), which came into force in 1998 as part of the ATS. Article 7 of the Protocol declares that 'any activity relating to mineral resources other than scientific research shall be prohibited'. Environmentalists fear that the 'scientific research' exception could be exploited, just as the Japanese have allegedly carried out commercial whaling activities under the auspices of research. Even more uncertain is the protection or lack thereof of sensitive Antarctic ecosystems from commercial bio-prospecting activities. Bernard Herber (2006) worries that some version of an open-access 'national sovereignty solution' will emerge, rather than a 'global sovereignty' solution consistent with the deep-seabed segment of the LOSC. A minimal or laissez-faire regime such as that which presently exists for biological and genetic resources on the high seas would, he says, 'threaten the designation of Antarctica as a national reserve devoted to peace and science' (Herber, 2006: 145).

Conclusion

The Sovereignty Games narrative depicts a political world dominated by rivalries and the pursuit of self/national interest. Some commentators see this as relatively 'simple and predictable' (Hough, 2013: 14; Powell and Dodds, 2014: 11) compared to other geopolitical narratives. Viewed through this lens, the geopolitics of the deep takes the form of an ongoing contest for influence, power and resources among competing nation states with interests and aspirations for control of the oceans. This plays out geographically in the Arctic and Antarctic, the Indian Ocean, the South China Sea and on the high ocean. In contrast to the Saving the Ocean narrative discussed in the next chapter, the Sovereignty Games narrative privileges competition over collaboration, and free market sovereignty over the idea of a global commons (Duvall and Havercroft, 2009: 45–6). Nevertheless, international protocols such as the LOSC and the ATS do impose a measure of order in what might otherwise be a geopolitical free-for-all.

4

Saving the Ocean: Protecting the Commons

Wolfgang Friedmann, a visionary international legal scholar, expressed his increasing concern over the state of the deep in a book entitled *The Future of Oceans* (1971): 'The exploration and exploitation of growing portions of the ocean bed is already a fact – and one of growing international, economic, technological, and political importance' (Friedmann, 1971: 94). He noted the gradual conversion of the ocean bed from an area of 'mysteries and legends' to an 'explorable and exploitable area with a topography of mountains, ridges, slopes, plains, trenches and abysses' (Friedmann, 1971: 9). This changing geography of the deep set the stage for a quickening race to the bottom of the ocean in search of new sources of petroleum and other minerals, a trend, he predicted, which 'can only spell unmitigated disaster' (Friedmann, 1971: xi).[1] Previously, extractive resource exploitation referred almost exclusively to overfishing. Now, however, there was mounting evidence suggesting dramatic increases in the rates of extraction of both the non-living (petroleum, sand and gravel, marine minerals) and living (previously unexploited genetic materials) from marine environments, leading to fears that scarce and exhaustible resources would dissipate in a space of unregulated exploitation.

While environmentalists in the 1970s and 1980s occasionally decried the existence of offshore oil spills, toxic dumping, drift-net fishing and the decimation of whale and dolphin populations, mostly their concern focused on human impacts in shallow coastal waters. This should not be surprising, insofar as the inshore environment is more visible and familiar to the public, compared to deep-sea and open-ocean environments, which are generally out of sight and poorly understood (Baker et al., 2001: 5). The deep-sea floor of the high seas was not only off their radar, but, more often than not, it was 'deemed exploitable for biological resources and sea-floor minerals' (Ramirez-Llodra et al., 2011: 1).

As discussed in Chapter 2, a new international maritime regime began to form about the same time as Friedmann issued his warning about potential threats to the deep ocean. While the LOSC consistently makes reference to the escalating danger to deep-ocean ecosystems posed by weak regulatory mechanisms and structures, this was never intended to be its guiding brief. Rather, the 'common heritage of [hu]mankind' concept, the touchstone of the LOSC, was constructed more from the building blocks of equity and resource distribution than it was from considerations of deep-sea conservation. In short, it was not so much about 'saving' the commons as it was about 'sharing' it (Fatouros, 2006: 272–3).

This point of view continued to percolate, even after the LOSC was signed. For example, the 1998 Report of the Independent World Commission on the Oceans (*The Ocean . . . Our Future*) is generally regarded as a landmark statement of the importance of ocean conservation and sustainability. However, in keeping with the LOSC, the Report identified 'the quest for equity in the oceans' as an overarching challenge that must be addressed in determining the future directions of the oceans. Echoing Agenda 21 of the Rio Conference (1992 UN Conference on the Environment and Development), the Commission argued that greater equity in the oceans would contribute to reducing poverty and underdevelopment. Accordingly, 'the oceans should be seen as a domain where institutions and arrangements should contribute to accelerating the pace of social and economic development' (Soares, 1998: 55). While recognizing the environmental pressure on the oceans, the Report stresses that they 'continue to offer an immense source of wealth that could benefit all'.

Building support for the goal of increased equity in the oceans is said to be 'a formidable challenge' with many dimensions. Of these, one of the most important is the ability to command science and technology, since this is what distinguishes richer from poorer nations (Soares, 1998: 73). A good example of this is the joint development and sharing of technology for deep-ocean mining under the supervision of the ISA. If, as Adalberto Vallega (2001: 41) has observed, sustainability is a system constituted by three elements – ecosystem integrity, economic efficiency and social equity – then ocean governance has tipped the balance by privileging the third, social (and economic) equity.

Despite this preoccupation with engineering a more equitable distribution of the wealth of the ocean frontier, a fourth narrative, 'Saving the Ocean', has taken centre stage in recent years.

The deep sea, this discourse begins, is the largest ecosystem on earth and the ocean depths are home to a variety of life forms approaching that of tropical rainforests (Roberts et al., 2005: 1). Sadly, ocean ecosystems increasingly have come under serious threat. Assessing the state of the oceans on the twentieth anniversary of the 1992 UNCED meeting in Rio de Janeiro ('Rio Conference'), Susan Lieberman and Joan Yang of the Pew Environment Group (the conservation arm of the Pew Charitable Trusts) observe, 'Many have come to realize the fragile nature of ocean ecosystems. Once thought to be vast, resilient areas, able to absorb waste and withstand increased human population, fishing and shipping pressures, these ecosystems are increasingly showing their vulnerability' (Lieberman and Yang, 2013: 68). Some issues that negatively impact ocean ecosystems – for example, coastal development leading to the destruction of mangroves – are not directly applicable to the deep. Many others are profoundly so. The latter include both broad challenges and threats that have been raised at successive meetings within the United Nations system – climate change and ocean acidification; habitat and biodiversity loss; overfishing; and plastic marine pollution – and some new issues that pertain specifically to deep oceans – extraction of genetic material from marine life; and the future of seabed mining.

Threats to Deep-Water Ecosystems

In 2004, an invited team of international ocean scientists, economists, lawyers and conservationists gathered in Los Cabos, Mexico, to build a global action plan for ocean conservation. This 'Defying Ocean's End' conference was inspired 'by an urgent need – to address the sharp decline in ocean wildlife, the disturbing increase in ocean pollution and the neglect of policies and resources to solve these problems'. One of the theme groups at the meeting branded itself the 'Unknown Ocean' group. It set itself the task of considering several poorly known ocean environments with respect to the need for additional research and possible conservation action. After much discussion, the 'Unknown Ocean' group distinguished two categories of unknown habitats (Madin et al., 2004), most of which are located in the deep ocean. The first group includes four habitats 'with evidence of immediate conservation needs because the ecosystem is unique and valuable and is either already exposed to damaging human impacts or at high risk of such impacts in the near future' (Madin et al., 2004: 215). They are seamounts, deep and remote coral reefs, canyon and seep environments of the continental margin, and marine underground and underwater cave environments. The second group of six habitats are 'places in the ocean with significant ecological importance but for which there is some combination of insufficient data to assess conservation needs, no apparent human impact in the foreseeable future or no apparent mechanism to put conservation measures in place' (Madin et al., 2004: 215). They are the open-ocean water column; the deep-sea benthos (sea floor); ridge and vent ecosystems; polar seas and ice-edge zones; fronts and upwelling regions; and prokaryote (microbial) communities throughout the world's oceans.

The 'Unknown Ocean' theme group's assessment of these remote habitats provides a useful checklist of environmental threats to the deep ocean. Seamounts (isolated submarine mountains that rise to an elevation of a kilometre or more above the ocean floor) are increasingly under threat from deep-sea fishing activities. Deep and remote coral reefs can be subject to overfishing and disintegration related to global warming. Continental margins/slopes (boundary zones between the shallow shelf regions that surround most continents and the deeper, abyssal plains of the sea floor), underwater canyons and cold seeps (where colder sulphide and methane-rich fluids bleed from the deep sea floor) are or may soon be under threat from pollution, oil exploitation, waste disposal and overfishing. Underground and underwater cave environments (they are called anchialine habitats) are at great risk from a number of human activities: vandalism; souvenir collecting; dumping of trash; quarrying; cesspit leakage; deep-well injection of wastes; construction work; and the drilling of water wells above or near caves.

The second group of unknown habitats for which the biodiversity and ecological structures are relatively unknown 'are all areas that have great significance to the overall stability of the global ocean ecosystem and the planet as a whole' (Madin et al., 2004: 230). The open-ocean water column plays a significant role in removing carbon dioxide from the atmosphere but appears to be negatively affected by increasing ocean acidification. Additionally, the removal of top predator fish by high-seas fishing may disrupt complex microbial communities. Deep-sea benthos (sea-floor habitats) could be at risk from manganese nodule mining, ocean dumping of radioactive and other wastes, and carbon sequestration (carbon capture storage) projects. Ridge and (hydrothermal) vent systems are vulnerable to damage and ecological disruption from the mining of polymetallic sulphides (see below). Frozen seas and ice edges are seasonal habitats that appear to be undergoing change from climate warming. Fronts and upwelling zones can occur at the boundaries of major currents in the open sea. Insofar as they are important feeding areas for large pelagic fish, overfishing can be lethal. Finally, microbial communities are the biogeochemical foundation of all ecosystems on earth, both marine and terrestrial. While their diversity and ecology are poorly understood, there is great concern that a suite of harmful human impacts could combine to impair their functioning.

Rather than consider environmental threats to deep-sea environments according to the type of habitat, another approach is to organize this on the basis of the human activity that generates the risk. Using this method, there are seven main categories of threat: deep-water fisheries; mining; oil and gas drilling; carbon sequestration; ocean acidification; waste disposal and dumping; and exploitation of methane hydrates.

Deep-Water Fisheries

Fishing constitutes a paradox. On the one hand, it clearly represents *the* predominant threat to deep-water water ecosystems today. The environmental group Oceana calls commercial trawling the most pervasive of all human activities in the deep sea, with some 40% of the world's trawling grounds situated in waters deeper than the continental shelf from depths of 200 to 1,800 metres (Roberts et al., 2005: 14). An increasing proportion of species are now being caught from seamounts, rather than on the continental slope. According to a 2012 policy paper commissioned by the Pew Environment Group, the deep-sea fishing fleets around the world are causing significant harm to the ocean ecosystem: 'As currently practiced, deep-sea fishing has serious and widespread environmental consequences for deep-sea fishing countries, the international community and ocean ecosystems. . . . Such damage occurs through bottom contact with fragile habitats and the overfishing of highly vulnerable deep-sea species' (Pew Environment Group, 2012: 2). It should come as no surprise that the final report of the Global Ocean Commission primarily addressed issues pertaining to deep fisheries.

On the other hand, any extended consideration of fishing has been next to invisible in the Oceanic Frontiers narrative discussed in Chapter 1 of this book. As we have seen, in the books and articles churned out by 'ocean boosters' such as Arthur C. Clarke and Robert Cowen in the 1950s and early 1960s fishing was front and centre in the 'promise of plenty' promised by the exploitation of the global seas. Since then, however, this has taken a back seat to the contributions of mining, oil and gas drilling and bio-prospecting. One possibility is that, despite its relatively high profile as an environmental issue, deep-sea fishing has not been especially lucrative. The Pew report (Pew Environment Group, 2012: 2) states that 'deep-sea fisheries are of little economic importance', accounting for just 2 to 4% of the worldwide catch ('world landings'). In part, this may reflect the fact that since deep-water fisheries began to operate commercially in the 1960s and 1970s, a number of species have become depleted and are not expected to recover.

There are several factors that account for the growth of deep-water fisheries from the 1960s onwards. Improving fishing technologies clearly played a major role. The industry developed stronger net materials, more powerful engines and winches and better fish-finding electronics, enabling these fisheries to expand into deeper and deeper waters (Roberts et al., 2005: 14). These technological developments have made net fishing much more lethal. For example, nets made from synthetic fibres last longer, require less maintenance and result in larger catches because they are much less visible to fish. They need not be retrieved as often. As a result, new microfilament nets 'move around the ocean for years as "ghost nets," damaging ecosystems and killing fish that then cannot be used for human consumption or cannot reproduce to help replenish fish stocks' (DeSombre and Barkin, 2011: 42).

Technological innovation has also facilitated the creation of highly destructive new methods of deep-ocean trawling and longlining. Longline fisheries are used particularly in areas where trawlers cannot easily go as a result of rocky outcrops, rugged terrain such as seamounts and canyons, or fisheries regulations (Ramirez-Llodra et al., 2011: 10). Longlines can be tens of miles long, carry thousands of hooks and catch far more than the target species (Roberts, 2012: 323). Traditional fishing grounds have become less attractive as a result of declining fish stocks, increasing regulation and the advent of EEZs in many continental shelf areas, with the result that vessels are compelled to explore progressively deeper and more distant waters and new species of fish (Ramirez-Llodra et al., 2011: 9). Scientists know relatively little about deep-sea species such as the roundnose grenadier, orange roughy and Patagonian tooth fish (also known as the Chilean sea bass), but fear that they will face extinction without some form of regulatory regime (Freestone, 2007: 534).

In addition to the threat of fish extinction, commercial trawling poses a number of other threats to deep-sea ecosystems. The most visible effects are observed for the sea floor on and around seamounts, where heavy fishing results in almost a complete loss of communities of slow-growing sea-floor animals such as corals and sponges. Recovery here may take centuries. Insofar as corals and sponges provide a living habitat to other species, their loss could trigger domino effects for much of the local ecology of the seamount or seamount chain (Roberts et al., 2005: 16). Bottom trawling, Robin Abadia and her co-authors (2004: 185) report, 'has been compared to harvesting vegetables with a bulldozer or clear-cutting the rainforest'.

Ocean Mining

In assessing magnitude and probability of threats to deep-sea ecosystems, Oceana observes, 'If mining becomes common in the future, it could pose the greatest and most widespread threat to deep sea communities of all human activities' (Roberts et al., 2005: 19). That said, Oceana allows that the environmental impacts of mining in the deep sea are currently not well understood. Rod Fujita (2003: 165–6) points out that the environmental impacts of ocean mining, while difficult to predict, generally depend on the kind of mining that takes place, and where this occurs. Peter Herzig, an economic geologist who directs GEOMAR, a large ocean-research centre in Kiel, Germany, and serves as President of the International Partnership for the Observation of the Ocean, told a Toronto audience in March 2013 that he was not concerned about sulphide mining, but he would most certainly not like to see manganese nodule mining (Herzig, 2013).

We have a pretty good idea that mining for manganese nodules on the seabed will prove to be problematic. This is likely to result in 'vast plumes of re-suspended sediment that could choke biological communities for miles around' (Herzig, 2013). Herzig notes that the dust storm kicked up by va-cuuming the seabed for manganese nodules takes days to settle. Manganese nodule mining, he says, will have an environmental effect not just at the mining site but *on the entire ocean*.

The consequences of mining for polymetallic sulphide deposits near hydrothermal vents are less well understood.

On the one hand, mining near the vents would probably result in less re-suspension of sediments because the mineral deposits are relatively new and generally covered with thin layers of sediments (Fujita, 2003: 165). Furthermore, the more adaptable and ephemeral biological communities on vents might be expected to re-colonize more quickly than the slower-growing animal communities on the continental slopes and abyssal plains. On the other hand, there may be considerable potential for ecological disruption. For example, the mining process, probably some variation on strip mining and open-cast mining, could release toxic metals that would harm marine food webs. Also, accidental damage to conveyance systems bringing ore to the surface could lead to catastrophic toxicity and the burial of organisms (Fujita, 2003: 165).

Deep-Water Oil and Gas Drilling

Drilling for oil and gas in ultra-deep-water environments – those over 1,500 metres of water depth – in Brazil, the Gulf of Mexico and the Gulf of Guinea represents a potentially lucrative activity carried out on the 'frontier of extraction', one that represents a feature of the international political economy of oil (Bridge and Le Billon, 2013: 13–14). As an environmental problem, it is significant because we really do not know very much about what will happen and what to do if something goes wrong. This was dramatically illustrated in the 2010 Deepwater Horizon blowout in the Gulf of Mexico. Even though there had been some massive well failures in the past, the Deepwater spill was different because it occurred over 1,500 metres below water rather than at around 90 metres. Deepwater Horizon, Callum Roberts (2012: 133) writes, taught us several things: 'We know now how much harder it is to contain a spill at depth than in the shallows. And we know that we are extraordinarily unprepared for problems at the deepening frontier of oil and mineral exploitation. . . . The disaster taught us that spilled oil doesn't always bubble to the surface as everyone expected.' Long after the well was capped, plenty of oil remained far below the surface of the ocean, along with 700,000 gallons of chemical dispersant that BP injected at the leaking wellhead (Roberts, 2012: 134).

According to Oceana, oil- and gas-drilling activities are considered to have the greatest effect next to trawling and other fisheries activities among potential threats to deep-sea ecosystems. This threat is magnified further because more than 40% of the entire ocean is now within drilling depth (Roberts et al., 2005: 18).

As the Deepwater disaster in the Gulf of Mexico illustrates, oil and gas spills present a formidable threat to the coastal marine environment. What is less well understood is what happens when oil and gas are released in the extremely cold, high-pressure environment of the deep sea (Helvarg, 2006: 115). Initially, it was thought that production of petroleum from the deep-ocean floor was unlikely to be as problematic as it is for confined coastal areas or near-offshore environments because they are located far from the shores and continental shelf regions where 95% of the world's fish is caught (Emery, 1979: 92). More recently, however, some troubling concerns have been raised. In December 2010, a research cruise was organized using the WHOI submersible *Alvin* to gauge the damage to seep communities from the spill. First observations showed colonies of coral at 1,400 metres depth were recently dead or dying (Ramirez-Llodra et al., 2011: 13). Another threat may come from oil-drilling muds, which have been shown to be toxic to corals and to inhibit the settlement of invertebrate larvae in shallow waters. This may prove to be an even more serious problem in the deep sea, where biotic communities have lower resistance, as well as slower recovery rates (Roberts et al., 2005: 18).

Carbon Sequestration

Carbon capture storage (CCS) consists of a series of technologies that enable the capture of carbon dioxide (CO_2) from power plants or industrial installations. Projects of this type are more advanced on land than in the ocean – the world's first commercial-scale carbon capture and storage project fired up in the province of Alberta, Canada, on 2 October 2014. Offshore, CO_2 is ideally compressed and transported in liquefied form to a deep geological formation under the seabed, where it is stored for hundreds of years (Armeni, 2013: 3; Milligan, 2014: 162). Environmentalists are somewhat conflicted over whether this should be encouraged. On the one hand, CCS methods promise to remove CO_2 from the atmosphere. However, the environmental cost of this may be damage caused by leakage of captured CO_2 from storage sites. Similarly, there may be negative ecological impacts from an alternative CCS method that would directly dispose of liquid CO_2 onto the seabed surface.

To date, there are several operational projects, both of which store carbon dioxide in depleted oil and gas reservoirs. The longest established of these (since October 1996) is located in the Sleipner gas fields in the North Sea. The Sleipner plant has stored about 1 million tons of CO_2 at a depth of 800–1,000 metres below the sea floor. A similar project in the Snohvit gas field in the Barents Sea stores 700,000 tons per year at a depth of 320 metres. Both of these are relatively small-scale when compared to proposed industrial-scale CO_2 disposal, which would store about 1,000 times this amount (Ramirez-Llodra et al., 2011: 9).

Ocean Acidification

Ocean acidification is often referred to as 'the other CO_2 problem'. Jean-Pierre Gattuso and Lina Hansson (2011), the authors of one recent textbook on the subject, observe that ocean acidification has stood in the shadow of global warming for many years. Note, for example, that the coverage of ocean acidification in the Fourth Assessment Report of the Intergovernmental Panel on Climate Change (IPCC) published in 2007 comprised only a few pages out of a total of several thousand. Recently, however, ocean acidification 'is beginning to gain increased consideration for policy-makers, politicians, the media and the general public' (Gattuso and Hansson, 2011: 13). Notably, Sir Mark Walport, the UK's Chief Scientific Adviser, told BBC News that the current rate of acidification is believed to be unprecedented within the last 65 million years – and may threaten fisheries in the future. 'If we carry on emitting CO_2 at the same rate,' Walport warns, 'ocean acidification will create substantial risks to complex marine food webs and ecosystems' (Harrabin, 2014).

Under normal conditions, the ocean absorbs a significant portion of CO_2 emissions from human activities, meaning that it acts as a 'sink'. This is roughly equivalent to about one-third of the total emissions from the past 200 years. Some of this is utilized by photosynthesis. However, a much greater proportion is removed from the surface by thermohaline sinking – a system of deep currents dependent on temperature and salinity, whereby warm surface water is cooled and sinks to the deep basins of the global ocean (McGowan and Field, 2002: 11, 25). The result constitutes a kind of trade-off. As the (US) National Research Council (2010: 1) explains, 'Uptake of CO_2 by the ocean benefits society by moderating the rate of climate change, but this also causes unprecedented changes to ocean chemistry, decreasing the pH of the water[2] and leading to a suite of chemical changes collectively known as ocean acidification.' What transpires is the progressive alteration of seawater chemistry caused by uptake of atmospheric CO_2. Increased CO_2 concentrations and the accompanying changes in ocean chemistry may alter species composition, abundance and health (Cooley and Mathis, 2013: 34). The word 'may' is used here because we do not really know exactly what effects ocean acidification will have on deep-sea ecosystems. As Eva Ramirez-Llodra and her co-authors (2011: 15) explain, 'In contrast to the previous examples of human impact on the deep-sea, where there are measurable data, much of our understanding of the impact of climate change is speculative, in part because there are only a few sites with the long-term baseline data needed to document biological changes.'

Nevertheless, it is possible to identify some probable effects of increasing ocean acidification. At the level of individual species, this will be likely to result in ecological 'winners' and 'losers' (Cooley and Mathis, 2013: 35). Chief among the former are 'calcifying' marine animals (i.e. those with shells), for example molluscs, that rely on obtaining argonite, a common calcium carbonate compound that is quite soluble. Inadequate shell building can, among other things, increase or prolong their exposure to predators. Also at risk are stony corals and other deep-water corals. The latter are important because they contribute to deep-water diversity and provide a habitat for a variety of other species (Ramirez-Llodra et al., 2011: 15). Researchers from the University of Exeter recently reported another, potentially more widespread negative effect of ocean acidification. As acidity increases, it creates conditions for animals to take up more coastal pollutants such as copper. The Exeter scientific team reports that at the pH expected by the end of the century, sea urchins, a keystone species, will face damage from copper to 10% of their DNA. Exeter biologist Ceri Lewis told BBC environment analyst Roger Harrabin, 'It's a bit of a shock frankly. . . . It means the effects of ocean acidification may be even more serious than we previously thought. We need to look with new eyes at things which we thought were not vulnerable' (Harrabin, 2014).

On the other hand, some species are accustomed to environments where the pH level is naturally high (e.g. volcanic CO_2 vents) or varies over a wide range. In this situation, there may be a wholesale shift in the ecosystem, with some keystone species migrating to a more suitable habitat (Cooley and Mathis, 2013: 36). This appears to have occurred in the North Pacific in 1977 and 1989 (Hare and Mantua, 2000). Furthermore, ocean acidification seems to take place in lockstep with other processes, notably warming, reduced oxygenation (decline in oxygen) and the localized release of methane. Together, these could have the effect of radically altering the structure of deep-sea biological communities.

Waste Disposal and Dumping

It is usual to distinguish between two types of marine debris: floating litter and seabed litter. Not surprisingly, much more is known about the former. Nevertheless, impacts of litter on deep-sea habitats are many, including: the suffocation of animals from plastics; release of toxic chemicals; introduction and propagation of invasive species; and physical damage to cold-water corals (Ramirez-Llodra et al., 2011: 6). The United Nations Environment Programme (UNEP) estimates that plastic waste alone kills up to 1 million sea birds, 100,000 sea mammals and countless fish each year (Gjerde, 2006: 54).

Callum Roberts (2012: 162–3) identifies an increasingly worrisome situation whereby many of the plastic particles in the oceans range from a few hundredths to a few thousandths of an inch in size. For example, cosmetics manufacturers now add tiny plastic granules to hand lotions and face creams as exfoliants that are too small to be filtered out by sewage treatment plants. These are washed out to sea, where they are ingested by plankton, which mistake them for food. Plankton are an essential part of the diet of certain fish, meaning that plastic moves upwards in the food chain.

Methane Hydrates

In Chapter 1, we discussed the vast potential of methane hydrates as an energy resource. At the same time as hydrates are imagined as being a 'potential panacea for an energy-hungry planet' (Monroe, 2005: 6), they may also constitute a natural hazard of considerable concern. This has much to do with their inherent instability. Some scientists have warned that decomposing hydrates can trigger undersea landslides and even a large-scale tsunami. One problem may be the collapse of undersea slopes as a result of hydrate decomposition. Neal Driscoll and his colleagues (2000) speculate that the outer shelf off southern Virginia and North Carolina might be in the initial stages of a large-scale slope failure, raising the possibility that a tsunami equivalent to the storm surge spawned by a category three or four hurricane will envelop the nearby coastal zone. As the methane gas from hydrate decomposition makes its way to the ocean surface, it could become a major climate destabilizer, precipitating a sharp warming trend. One theory suggests that the first appearance of many modern land mammal species 55 million years ago was due to such a warming event prompted by a methane release from displaced hydrates. Conversely, changes in the temperature of the world's oceans could alter the low temperatures hydrates need to exist near the sea floor, causing them to decompose and thus setting in motion the series of catastrophic events described above (Driscoll et al., 2000: 6).

Constructing the Saving the Ocean Narrative

To successfully construct and market a collective claim involving an environmental situation deemed to be problematic, there are three key tasks which must be carried out: assembling, presenting and contesting (Hannigan, 2014). Assembling requires that the problem be discovered, named, elaborated and legitimated. With global environmental issues this occurs most often in the realm of science. Presenting requires that the situation be brought to the attention of the world at large as worthy of public attention and concern. This usually occurs in the realm of mass media. Finally, if meaningful action is to be taken to mitigate or remedy the problem, it must be contested, which means translated into political action.

Friends of the ocean are convinced that the ecosystem of the deep is facing a serious crisis if we do not act promptly and decisively face multiple challenges. First of all, it is necessary to tackle the problem of issue distinctiveness. Not only must the dangers facing deep-sea flora and fauna be separated out from environmental problems as a whole, but they also need to be distinguished from global threats to the oceans that focus mainly on coastal and near-shore areas. This is often difficult because, despite the efforts of state and non-state actors to make the deep 'legible', ocean space is fundamentally continuous and indivisible. At the same time, some threats to the oceans – for example, the use of trawling technologies in industrial fishing – apply to both the surface ocean and the deep. Second, when it comes to the discourse of the deep, the Saving the Ocean narrative is not the only game in town. That is, it must compete with the other three narratives discussed in this book for attention and legitimacy.

In the 1970s and 1980s, biodiversity loss captured wide public attention in part owing to the establishment of 'conservation biology'. Conservation biology, an applied science that studies biodiversity and the dynamics of extinction, differs from other natural resource fields such as wildlife management, fisheries and forestry by accenting ecology over economics (Grumbine, 1992: 29). With the creation of the

Society for Conservation Biology in 1985, conservation was formally recognized as an academic discipline. Conservation biology has provided an academic nesting spot for research on biodiversity loss. It is a 'crisis discipline', meaning that it provides the intellectual and technological tools with which to take aggressive conservation action. Furthermore, it draws its content and methods from a broad range of fields within and outside of the biological sciences (Hannigan, 2014: 159). In assembling the Saving the Ocean narrative as both distinctive and important, we must recognize the vital contribution of two academic specialties: biological oceanography (notably deep-sea biology) and ecological economics.

Biology at the Ocean Extremes[3]

Until quite recently, our knowledge of the deep ocean remained very elementary. Most scientists assumed that the sea floor was a vast plain, empty and still – almost devoid of life, even without currents (Roberts et al., 2005: 2). Granted, a century of oceanographic studies, beginning with the *Challenger* expedition (see Chapter 1), had conclusively dispelled the 'azoic hypothesis' (i.e. that no life exists below around 500 metres). Nevertheless, understanding of deep oceans remained sorely limited: the deep was thought to be a zone of low biodiversity, no primary production, no seasonality – in short, a uniformly cold, food-poor, dark, tranquil and invariant environment (Ramirez-Llodra et al., 2011: 1).

To a considerable degree, this perception can be traced to a major error perpetuated by Charles Wyville Thomson, the leader of the *Challenger* expedition. Thomson wrongly believed that with increasing depth there was a decrease in the variety of animal life, that is, species richness or diversity. That he came to this conclusion is quite understandable. Mostly, what the *Challenger* crew collected in their trawls and dredges were large, surface-dwelling marine animals such as sea cucumbers, sea urchins and molluscs. Since sea-floor animals generally become smaller with increasing depth, the *Challenger* samples were non-representative. Thomson's conclusion about the inverse relationship between ocean depth and biodiversity was perpetuated for more than eight decades after the expedition; as late as 1954, the main textbook in the field stated that with increasing distance from land (and therefore with increasing depth) you found ever fewer species (Tyler et al., 2001: 262–3).

This stark picture has since been dispelled by three decades of marine research, most notably in the discipline of biological oceanography. Biological oceanography[4] is the study of marine organisms, their relationships and their interactions with their geochemical and physical environment. It focuses on the abundance, variety and distribution of life in the sea (DeLong and Ward, 1992: 47). Biological oceanography has a strong applied environmental character. David Caron (1992: 16–17) describes the field as playing a central role in assessing human impact on the environment, a contribution that is sure to grow in importance as human encroachment on the marine environment increases. Researchers in biological oceanography, he says, 'strive to understand how the ocean functions, define the limits of its abilities to absorb our activities, and assure that we do not exceed these limits'. Ultimately, this knowledge is critical to the continued health of the ocean, the planet, and our own future.

The 'new age of deep-sea biology' was initiated in the mid-1960s, but did not really blossom until several decades later. A major contributing factor was the development of new types of sampling equipment that were much more sensitive than the dredges and trawls that had been used for so long to bring up marine samples from the ocean depths. Another technological breakthrough was the use of deep-sea submersibles that allowed direct observation and experimentation at the deep-seabed (Tyler et al., 2001: 264). Together, these innovations directed scientific attention to the surprising diversity of life to be found in the deep ocean, and, by implication, to the impending human threat to this diversity.

Italian geographer Adalberto Vallega (2001) has suggested that the largely unrecognized, true legacy of the United Nations Conference on Environment and Development (UNCED, 3–14 June 1992) can be found in its holistic approach. More specifically, he points to its achievement of replacing the concept of the 'environment', which had supported the vision of the earlier (1972) UN Conference on the

Human Environment, with that of the 'ecosystem'. A key event here is the adoption of the CBD, which entered into force on 29 December 1993 and 'marks the rise of the biological sciences as the leading disciplines influencing political policy aimed at sustainable development' (Vallega, 2001: 41). Biodiversity is a central concern of both UNCED and the CBD. At the level of 'species diversity', it becomes a key concept in ocean management insofar as it 'shows the degree of complexity of an ecosystem' (Vallega, 2001: 46).

This growing recognition of the importance of ecosystems, species diversity and the biological sciences provides deep-ocean activists with a useful narrative hook. Referring specifically to the Antarctic, Bernard Herber (2006: 140) writes, 'Since a "positive" correlation exists between biodiversity and the stability of ecosystems, while a "negative" correlation exists between biodiversity and economic production, it must be concluded that the fragile ecology of Antarctica is extremely sensitive to activities such as unregulated bioprospecting that could disrupt its biodiversity in a significant manner.' The same 'inextricable factual link' exists, Herber (2006: 142) says, 'between the protection of the deep seabed environment, including its biodiversity, marine scientific research and bioprospecting.'

One of the challenges of making ocean biodiversity (and biodiversity loss) 'legible' to environmental publics is to package it in familiar terms. Recognizing this, in the late 1990s, several leading marine scientists approached the Alfred P. Sloan Foundation expressing their concerns that 'humanity's understanding of what lives in the oceans lagged far behind our desire and need to know' (Gross, 2010: 147). In fact, ocean researchers themselves did not really know how many species of marine animals there were, where they were to be found and what their territorial range was. They proposed conducting a census 'to assess and explain the diversity, distribution and abundance of marine life' in all ocean realms from the near shore to the abyssal depths (Gross, 2010: 147). With financial and operational support from the Sloan Foundation, a handful of national government agencies and various NGOs, a *Census of Marine Life* was undertaken. It took a decade for more than 2,700 scientists to compile but the results were stunning. Christine Buckley (2010) notes, 'Before the advent of the Census, about 230,000 ocean species were known to science, but researchers estimate that two to three times this number actually exist. At least 5,300 new species have been discovered thus far in the Census.' Some of these previously unknown species are visually arresting: 'squid-worms' with strange-looking tentacles in the Celebes Sea; a blind lobster with a long, spiny pincer in the Philippines Sea; a furry crab in a vent off Easter Island; and eight-legged sea spiders in Antarctica much larger than any previously seen. Communities of marine species were discovered on the deep-sea floor and at the mouth of superheated hydrothermal vents and seeps – environments that were previously thought to be too severe to sustain life. According to the census, there may additionally be up to a billion types of microbes to be found in the sea.

Ecological Economics

Like biological oceanography, ecological economics draws from a wide variety of fields, in this case within and beyond the marine sciences. Unlike conservation biology, however, it attempts to fruitfully combine the differing methodologies of economics and ecology (Harris, 1995a: 50–1), rather than privileging one over the other. The core problem addressed in ecological economics is how to sustain the interactions between economic and ecological systems, a task that requires transcending the normal academic boundaries of the academic disciplines and the territorial boundaries of nation states (Costanza et al., 1999: 173).

Although its lineage can be traced back as far as the seventeenth century, ecological economics has its immediate roots in work carried out in the 1960s and 1970s by Nicholas Georgescu-Roegen, Herman Daly and Kenneth Boulding. In *The Entropy Law and the Economic Process* (1971) and other writing, Georgescu-Roegen challenges three fundamental assumptions that underpin the mathematical analysis of production by neoclassical economists: market systems are closed; non-market environmental resources (e.g. solar, water, wind) must be viewed as existing outside market systems and treated as externalities; and there are no limits on the growth and expansion of market economies (Nadeau, 2006: 138).

Daly, a World Bank economist and former student of Georgescu-Roegen's at Vanderbilt University, published a collection of articles titled *Toward a Steady-State Economy* (1973) that explored the question of whether perpetual growth was not only possible but morally desirable as well. The answer, Daly concluded, is 'no', especially 'in the context of the energy and environmental realities that we confront' (Cleveland, 1995: 32). Daly was largely responsible for introducing the linked concepts of 'scale' and 'limits' to debates on economic growth. Unlike neoclassical economics, which admits no scale limits, Daly argues that we are presently living in a 'bull-in-the-china-shop' economy, large enough to do significant damage to ecosystem resilience (the bounce-back capacity which allows ecosystems to recover from short-term damage or disruption) (Harris, 1995b: 98–9). The solution he proposes is to institute a 'steady-state economy', which would minimize the generation of 'throughput' (the use of resources and the generation of waste). Daly suggests three rules to help define the sustainable limits of throughput (Daly, 1990; Meadows et al., 1992: 46). For renewable resources, the sustainable rate of use can be no greater than the rate of regeneration. For non-renewable resources, the sustainable rate of use can be no greater than the rate at which a renewable resource, used sustainably, can be substituted for it. For a pollutant, the sustainable rate of emission can be no greater than the rate at which that pollutant can be recycled, absorbed or rendered harmless by the environment.

Boulding is best known for his article 'The Economics of the Coming Spaceship Earth' (1966). He argues that the open 'cowboy' or 'frontier' economy of the past is no longer viable. At current levels of usage, readily available supplies of fossil fuels will only last several centuries, or less if population growth continues to accelerate. This portends a 'closed' future for our planet. In suggesting an alternative, Boulding employs a metaphor in which the earth has become a 'spaceship'. In the spaceship, limited resources are available, as are reservoirs for waste disposal. The entire economy must be strictly managed here if humanity is to survive. As does Daly, Boulding says that the key to survival in the 'spaceship' or 'spaceman' economy is lessened throughput (production and consumption).

One link between these foundational studies in ecological economics and the Saving the Ocean narrative is to be found in the work of the Club of Rome. The Club is an international think tank or invisible college, founded in April 1968 at the instigation of the Italian industrialist and management consultant Aurelio Peccei. In the early 1970s, the Club commissioned Professor Jay Forrester's Systems Dynamics Group at MIT to undertake a two-year study of the long-term causes and consequences of growth in population, industrial capital, resource consumption and pollution. Using the World3 computer model, the MIT researchers, led by Dennis Meadows, projected seven scenarios or possible paths to the future. They concluded that many resource and pollution flows had grown beyond their sustainable limits. Unless population and the finite resources of the environment were brought into a state of equilibrium, the result would be 'overshoot' of the limits of growth, followed by uncontrolled decline. This raised the spectre of nothing less than the collapse of civilization itself and the advent of an exhausted and polluted planet (Harper, 2001: 293).

These results were summarized in *The Limits to Growth* (Meadows et al., 1972), a general non-technical book. *The Limits* was both controversial and widely noticed, selling 9 million copies in 29 languages. It became a key reference point in environmentalist writing throughout the 1970s (Hannigan, 2011: 44). While *The Limits to Growth* was not presented as a study in ecological economics per se, nevertheless its authors used a similar vocabulary to and arrived at the same general conclusions as Daly and Boulding. For example, in considering what a world of non-growth might be like, the authors propose the idea of an 'equilibrium state',[5] which they note parallels that discussed by a number of philosophers, economists and biologists in the past, including both Boulding (1966) and Herman Daly (1971).

One of the more active members of the Club of Rome was Elisabeth Mann Borgese. Borgese and Aurelio Peccei obviously held one another in high esteem. In his semi-biographical book *The Human Quality*, Peccei (1977: 186) praises Borgese: 'My dear friend Elisabeth Mann Borgese of the

Center for the Study of Democratic Institutions of Santa Barbara California, and leader of the "Pacem in Maribus" movement, is the one I most admire of those dedicated people, who, in and out of conferences, fight unsparingly for these ideas to be brought to fulfilment.' For her part, Borgese (1998: 6) comments in the Prologue to her book *The Oceanic Circle* (with a Foreword written by Club of Rome President Ricardo Diez-Hochleitner), 'The Club of Rome is well prepared to play a role in formulating and propagating a better understanding of the majesty of the oceanic circle.' Accordingly, the Club of Rome included a section authored by Borgese and Arvid Pardo on the emerging LOSC in its volume *Reshaping the International Order (RIO): A Report to the Club of Rome*, compiled under the direction of Nobel laureate Jan Tinbergen in 1976 (Tinbergen, 1977). That same year, the Club of Rome and the IOI (founded, as noted in Chapter 2 above, by Borgese) held a joint conference in Algiers to discuss the implications of the Tinbergen report, including the study on the Law of the Sea (Borgese, 1998: 8). While it could be argued that Borgese was ultimately more concerned with issues of global equity and good ocean governance than she was with ecological threats to the deep, nevertheless, some ecological economic thinking did find its way into her writing.

Another, more direct, link here is through the work of Robert Costanza. Costanza, an engineer, architect and systems ecologist, co-founded (with Daly) the Society for Ecological Economics in the 1980s and 'has been at least on the periphery of most of the important advances in ecological economics' (McKibben, 2007b: 27). In 1999, he was the lead author of the 'Introduction' to a special issue of the journal *Ecological Economics* devoted to the sustainable governance of oceans. This paper summarized and synthesized ideas contained in papers presented at an expert workshop convened in Lisbon, Portugal, on 7–9 July 1997 in order to provide advice on how ecological economics could assist in reaching the goal of sustainable governance of the oceans.

The Lisbon consensus underscored six major elements: a growing recognition of the ecological, economic and social dependence of sustainable human welfare on the oceans; a framework based on the value of the ecosystem for evaluating the major ocean problems (overfishing, land-based contamination, ocean disposal and spills, destruction of coastal ecosystems, climate change); an integrated ecological economic view of ocean governance; a set of six core principles for achieving governance of the oceans based on this perspective (i.e. the 'Lisbon principles'); an analysis of the major problems and threats to the oceans in terms of how they violate the Lisbon principles; and a set of possible solutions, including share-based fisheries, integrated watershed management, marine protected areas and environmental assurance bonds.

As has been noted, there are six Lisbon principles of sustainable governance: the *responsibility principle* (access to environmental resources carries attendant responsibilities to use them in an ecologically sustainable, economically efficient and socially fair manner); the *scale-matching principle* (appropriate scales of governance are those that maximize information about the relevant ecological system, respond quickly and efficiently and integrate across boundaries); the *precautionary principle* (if the risks of a potentially irreversible action are uncertain, err on the side of caution and do not proceed); the *adaptive management principle* (continual consultation between decision-makers with the goal of adaptive improvement); the *full cost allocation principle* (all external and internal costs and benefits of alternative decisions concerning the use of environmental resources should be identified, allocated and adjusted); and the *participation principle* (full stakeholder participation contributes to credible, accepted rules).

Marine Reserves

Whereas those who articulate the Governing the Abyss narrative emphasize how necessary it is to expand the Law of the Sea to include jurisdiction over biological and genetic resources, supporters of the Saving the Ocean narrative stress the value of marine reserves/marine protected areas for safeguarding ocean life and conserving biodiversity. In explaining why ocean zoning (the instrument used to create marine reserves) makes sense, Tundi Agardy (2010: 192), a marine conservationist and founder of the environmental NGO Sound Seas, observes, 'Ocean zoning is no panacea, but it is an extremely powerful tool that can force governments to go beyond endless planning to a marine management system that is strategic and adaptable.' Author Callum Roberts (2012: 294) calls marine reserves an indispensable building block of his 'New Deal for the oceans'. They are optimally designed to combat overfishing and to protect corals. By placing certain areas of the ocean off limits, marine reserves can boost the resilience of fish populations and fisheries. Ideally, they prove to be good breeding grounds and can bring back habitats that have been destroyed by trawls and dredges. Roberts believes that the spread and multiplication of marine protected areas is the best way to reach his ambitious target of protecting a third of the oceans from direct exploitation and harm (Roberts, 2012: 306), a huge jump from the present figure of only 1.6%. The best-known marine protected areas such as the Great Barrier Reef Marine Park in Australia tend to be located in coastal waters, but increasingly these are being established further out offshore.

In 1996, the Marine Conservation Institute and 1,605 marine scientists issued 'Troubled Waters: A Call for Action', calling on the world to protect 20% of every marine biogeographical region in order to save the sea's biodiversity. The Institute followed this up with an online 'Scientists' Letter Supporting Marine Reserves' (Marine Conservation Institute, 2014) to be sent to US President Barack Obama. Signatories (at last count 589 scientists had signed) include such celebrated names in marine exploration and science as Sylvia Earle, Callum Roberts and Carl Safina. The unprotected ocean, the letter says, is like a debit account where everybody withdraws and nobody deposits. By contrast, marine reserves *are like savings accounts that produce interest we can live off.* The letter enumerates a short list of benefits that accrue from marine protected areas:

> An extensive scientific literature now shows compelling evidence that strongly protected marine reserves are powerful

ways of conserving diversity. In addition, no-take reserves can create jobs and bring in new economic revenue through ecotourism and enhancement of local fisheries through spill-over beyond reserve boundaries. Finally, no-take reserves provide resilience against the impacts of climate change and ocean acidification.

The Most Pristine Place in the World

On 25 September 2014, US President Barack Obama signed a proclamation creating the largest marine reserve in the world completely off limits to commercial resource extraction including fishing. Invoking the Antiquities Act, first used by President Theodore ('Teddy') Roosevelt in 1906 to designate Devil's Tower National Monument in Wyoming, Obama expanded the Pacific Remote Islands Marine National Monu-ment to 490,000 square miles, about three times the size of California, and six times its current size. First created by President George W. Bush in January 2009 just before he left office, the Monument encompasses seven islands and numer-ous atolls and reefs peppering the south-central Pacific Ocean between Hawaii and American Samoa (Scharper, 2014). According to a Fact Sheet released by the Office of the White House Press Secretary, expanding the Monument, one of the most pristine marine environments in the world, will 'more fully protect the deep coral reefs, seamounts and marine eco-systems unique to this part of the world, which is also among the most vulnerable areas to the impacts of climate change and ocean acidification' (White House, 2014). The expanded Monument enlarges the current protected area from 40–51 to 130 seamounts,[6] underwater mountains that are hot spots of biodiversity.

Obama's Pacific initiative promises to be both less and more than it initially appears.

At first blush, it seems to signal the growing political pro-file and influence of the Saving the Ocean narrative and its proponents in the environmental NGO community. Scientific validation for the expansion was provided by a report, 'Expansion of US Pacific Remote Islands Marine National Monument: The Largest Ocean Legacy on Earth', prepared by Enric Sala, Lance Morgan, Elliott Norse and Alan Fried-lander (2014). Evidently, the authors were well pleased with Obama's plan. Sala, *National Geographic*'s 'explorer in residence', called the newly expanded Monument 'a great example of marine protection', while Norse, founder and chief scientist of the Seattle-based Marine Conservation Institute, exalted, 'What has happened is extraordinary. It is history making. There's a lot of reason[s] we should be celebrating right now' (Howard, 2014). Norse's colleague, Lance Morgan, President of the Marine Conservation Institute, concurred, 'We are pleased that President Obama proposed this bold action today – an action that will reverberate around the world – to expand and highly protect these amazing places that we first started working on in 2007' (Global Ocean Refuge System, 2014). Look more closely beyond this celebratory hype, however, and a more complex picture emerges.

While the huge area of the Pacific covered by the expanded Monument is pristine, there is no compelling evidence to suggest that it is critically threatened. The Report is under-whelming on this point. Consider, for example, its assessment of mining and oil and gas drilling:

> Given the geological history of the Pacific Basin, there are likely no oil and gas deposits in the region. For a number of years there has been discussion of mining cobalt crusts and manganese nodules from the basin and some limited exploration. No mineral extraction is currently taking place on the seafloor of the islands' EEZs. We believe seabed mining in the eight islands' EEZs would be incompatible with preserving these areas as intact, fully protected ecosystems. Therefore we recommend all minerals extraction be prohibited. (Sala et al., 2014: 28)

In a similar fashion, the Report adopts a 'precautionary' stance in regard to fishing. For example, evidence of illegal foreign fishing today is said to be largely anecdotal. The US Coast Guard observes the presence of about a dozen illegal fishing vessels per year in American island waters in the zone, although only one, an Ecuadorian boat, has been documented (but not apprehended). Nonetheless, a strong case can be made for conserving the Pacific Remote Islands 'because they harbor some of the best-preserved ocean habitats in the Pacific and are home to many species of key ecological and commercial importance' (Sala et al., 2014: 7). To be sure, the very fact that the assessment islands and their surrounding waters are some of the healthiest marine ecosystems remaining in the world, relatively intact and rich in biodiversity, gives them great scientific value, insofar as they serve both as a unique window into the past and as baselines for the future as to 'what "natural" islands and oceans are supposed to be' (Sala et al., 2014: 29).

For President Obama, expanding the US Pacific Remote Islands Marine National Monument provides a low-risk political opportunity to burnish his credentials and legacy as an environmental leader. Unlike the South China Sea or the Baltic, there are no armed fishing vessels or shadowy submarines to be reckoned with. Any other proposal to create even much smaller marine reserves around the US mainland or other islands would be received with strong opposition from the fishing lobby. Protection in the newly expanded Monument 'is not controversial because the islands are highly remote, under full US control, uninhabited, and principally used for conservation' (Sala et al., 2014: 4). Furthermore, as a *New York Times* (2014) editorial points out, 'Building an environmental legacy is an idea with bipartisan appeal.' This isn't entirely true – a few members of the US Congress opposed the expansion, citing the potential loss of commercial fishing grounds (Howard, 2014) – but protecting the oceans is much more likely to enjoy bipartisan appeal where it does not threaten too many powerful political or commercial interests.

Then, too, there may be some modest geopolitical gain abroad to be garnered here. Writing in the *Washington Post*, Juliet Eilperin (2014) asks, 'Why is Obama protecting a place you've never heard of?' One reason, she suggests, is that 'there's a global contest for bragging rights when it comes to marine reserves'. In expanding the Pacific Monument, the United States would trump Britain, which until March 2015 held the record for protecting the biggest swath of ocean: around the Chagos Islands, a military zone located in the

Indian Ocean approximately 310 miles south of the Maldives.[7] Eilperin cites Emily Woglom, Vice-President for Conservation and Policy at the Ocean Conservancy, who suggests that the President is now turning his attention to his 'Blue Legacy'. I doubt whether this 'global contest' plays much of a role in the sovereignty games discussed in Chapter 3 of this book. It could, however, help soften the ill feeling directed towards the United States by a number of nations for its alleged environmental sins, notably its refusal to buy into various international agreements on reducing carbon emissions.

What is perhaps as noteworthy as the US Pacific Remote Islands Marine National Monument expansion itself are the grounds used to justify it. The White House statement is peppered with references to the value of enhancing oceanic biodiversity and ecosystem integrity. This echoes the argument which I make earlier in this chapter that deep-sea biology only really began to take off as a scientific specialty area when it aligned itself with the diversity issue.

Equally important, Obama's proclamation taps into the mega-issue of global climate change. The 24 September 2014 White House Fact Sheet refers to both the 'Year of Action' and that May's National Climate Assessment:

> The recently released National Climate Assessment confirms that climate change is causing sea levels and ocean temperatures to rise. Changing temperatures can harm coral reefs and force certain species to migrate. In addition, carbon pollution is being absorbed by the oceans, causing them to acidify, which can damage coastal shellfish beds and reefs, altering entire marine ecosystems. To date, the acidity of our ocean is changing 50 times faster than any known change in millions of years. (White House, 2014)

Not that there appears to be any immediate threat by global climate change to the south-central Pacific Ocean. In fact, the scientific report that forms the basis for Obama's proclamation only mentions rising levels of atmospheric CO_2 and its impacts several times in passing, in the context of the Monument islands offering 'sites to monitor the effects of climate change on healthy ecosystems' (Sala et al., 2014: 29).

No matter, global climate change is on everyone's mind these days (see the next chapter), and if oceans are to occupy a more prominent place on the public policy radar, their relevance to climate change needs to be emphasized.

Conclusion

Saving the Ocean, our final discourse addressing the current condition and future state of the deep, overlaps to some extent with the Governing the Abyss narrative, but the thrust here is more explicitly ecological. While the latter is more inclined to validate seabed mining, as long as the forthcoming financial windfall and technology are shared with smaller nations, the former opposes it without qualification. Whereas the primary advocates and analysts of maritime governance are typically members of IGOs and/or legal scholars, the Saving the Ocean narrative is associated with biological oceanographers, ecological economists and environmental NGOs. The preferred 'management' strategy here is zoning the oceans, specifically the establishment of marine reserves and other marine protected areas.

Saving the Ocean appeals to policymakers because it skirts normal interest group politics surrounding the environment. This is illustrated by the uniformly positive reaction to the announcement of the creation of the Pitcairn Islands Marine Protected Area. Robin Lane Fox, the *Financial Times* gardening columnist, calls this 'the most ecologically friendly legislation from any party in British history' (Fox, 2015: 11). Promoted by a broad coalition of charities and pressure groups (the National Geographic Society, the Pew Charitable Trust, the Blue Marine Foundation) and celebrity advocates, notably actress Helena Bonham Carter, marine conservation zones secured full support from David Cameron's UK government, which was under fire for its land-based policies, notably its support of fracking (shale gas drilling). In his piece, Fox offers up a fresh way of framing marine reserve initiatives such as that created around the Pitcairn Islands. Marine conservation areas, he ventures, are 'Britain's underwater gardens, even more photogenic than the roses at the Chelsea Flower

Show' (Fox, 2015: 1). More of the plant life in Britain's overseas territory is underwater than above it. Note, however, that this botanic idyll is not entirely free of geopolitical vulnerabilities, as evidenced by the controversy surrounding the erstwhile Chagos Islands marine reserve (see note 7). Nonetheless, Saving the Ocean is presented as something akin to the longtime initiative in Britain to conserve and preserve birds, gardens and the countryside.

Conclusion: Global Climate Change and the Future of Deep Oceans

In this book, I have argued that almost everything about the sub-surface ocean – its definition, boundaries, value, ownership, health and future state – has been shaped by four master narratives: Oceanic Frontiers; Governing the Abyss; Sovereignty Games; and Saving the Ocean. While today these coexist and even frequently overlap, it is possible to situate each in a rough chronological order, each denoting a different kind of dominant framing of oceanic space.

In the decades immediately following World War II, the optimistic view that technological progress would lead to a better world centrally shaped our way of looking at the seven seas. Fuelled by the predictions of 'ocean boosters' such as the celebrated science fiction authors Arthur C. Clarke and Isaac Asimov, the deep was imagined as the 'next frontier' that would relieve the pressures of overpopulation; produce a bountiful source of food; and provide an unlimited source of oil, gas and precious minerals. These dreams were put on hold by the Cold War. With the launching of *Sputnik*, the oceans reverted to their World War II role as a medium for underwater surveillance and political gamesmanship by the superpower nations. Oceanography flourished, but only because research ships and submersibles were judged by navies to be useful in locating and raising sunken submarines and weapons of mass destruction. In the 1970s, agitation for the establishment of a New International Economic Order, combined with escalating jurisdictional disputes over fishing, oil drilling, ownership of Antarctica's resources and potential deep-sea mining, led to calls for a radically updated Law of the Sea. It took the better part of two decades, but a new international structure for governing the abyss was finally put in place in the form of the UN Law of the Sea Convention (LOSC), and its entry into force in 1994. By then, it was becoming ever more apparent that the ocean, including the deep, was coming under increasing threat from acidification, marine dumping, overfishing, offshore oil and gas drilling and, in the near future, mining and bio-prospecting. This came just as deep-sea biologists were discovering amazing new ecosystems far below the surface around seamounts, hydrothermal vents and cold seeps. Scientists and environmental crusaders combined forces to campaign for marine reserves and other protected areas to save biologically diverse species and ecological hot spots around the globe.

Climate Change and the Oceans

A new narrative of the deep oceans is emerging. This imagines oceans as a sort of 'canary-in-the-mineshaft' for gauging the impacts of global climate change. The climate change–oceans nexus is described by the text of a formal call for participation in the upcoming Third International Symposium on the Effects of Climate Change on the World Oceans, which was held in Santos City, Brazil, in March 2015:

> The Earth's climate is changing at a time when society re-evaluates its relationship with nature and with the services that natural systems provide to human societies. Oceans are central to the climate system, recycling half of the oxygen we breathe and absorbing half of the carbon dioxide we emit through the burning of fossil fuels. Oceans accumulate 97% of the Earth's water and 95% of all mobile carbon, providing food and livelihood opportunities to secure our well-being. Discussing the effects of climate change on the world's oceans is thus critical to understanding what is changing, how is it changing and how these changes will influence society. Direct and indirect effects of climate change on the marine

environment are already visible, but others can only be projected based on enhanced observations, experimentations and modeling efforts. We still have a rudimentary understanding of the sensitivity, vulnerability and adaptability of natural and managed marine ecosystems to climate change.[1]

This re-imagining of deep oceans incorporates various narrative threads. One sees the oceans as a type of early-warning system for droughts, floods and other environmental disasters, all of which are said by some scientists to be triggered or amplified by global warming. According to Trevor Platt, a marine biologist with the Partnership for Observation of Global Oceans (POGO),[2] scientists are urging governments around the world to invest in an ocean-based system of devices that would monitor the ocean's 'vital signs'. This proposed $15 billion system could do everything from indicating changes in fish populations to measuring how acidic the ocean is becoming in a certain region (*Metro* (Toronto), 2010).

Another story thread looks to the deep ocean to provide answers to thorny questions about global warming which have heretofore eluded mainstream atmospheric scientists and climate modellers. This is illustrated by what has come to be called the 'Mystery of Earth's Missing Heat'.

The 'Missing Heat' Debate

One of the major mysteries in the global climate change debate is why world air temperatures levelled off in the decade 2000–10, even though greenhouse gas emissions kept increasing. This question has been crucial. A failure to account for the 'missing heat' would provide ammunition to those who have been sceptical of the mainstream scientific argument that a steady rise in global mean temperatures is inevitable if measures are not taken immediately to reduce human-generated carbon emissions. Kevin Trenberth, a climate scientist at the National Center for Atmospheric Research in Boulder, Colorado, who is a strong advocate of the human-induced global warming thesis, famously remarked, 'The fact is that we can't account for the lack of warming at the moment and it is a travesty that we can't' (cited in Pearce, 2010: xiii).

Various influences – fluctuations in solar radiation, volcanic eruptions – have been suggested to explain this, but the jury is still out.

Then, near the end of the decade, another solution to the mystery was proposed by climate scientists. The 'missing heat', they said, was buried in layers of ocean deeper than 300 metres during periods like the past decade when air temperatures failed to rise as much as they might have (Zabarenko, 2011). Trenberth broached this possibility on a National Public Radio programme entitled 'The Mystery of Global Warming's Missing Heat' (Harris, 2008) and followed up with several scholarly articles. The landmark piece of research here was published by Sydney Levitus, Director of the World Data Center for Oceanography, and author of the *Climatological Atlas of the World Ocean* (1982). Levitus and his colleagues at NOAA used data from the World Oceans Database 2009, plus additional data processed to the end of 2010. They reported that each major ocean basin has warmed at nearly all latitudes, despite the variability produced by phenomena such as the El Niño–Southern Oscillation, the Pacific Decadal Oscillation and the North Atlantic Oscillation (Levitus et al., 2012). In fact, this has been occurring in the global ocean for just over half-a-century. The researchers note that immense ocean heating has not slowed in recent years – more of it has simply gone into the deeper ocean layers. Although surface warming has declined, global warming has not magically vanished, they insist, and the heat stored in the oceans will eventually come back to haunt us.

To test this hypothesis, Trenberth and his colleagues at the National Center for Atmospheric Research ran five computer simulations of global temperatures that indicated that an overall warming trend is expected to continue throughout this century. However, there would be periods when the temperatures would fall for a few years, before continuing their upwards climb. During these periods, the extra heat would move into deep ocean water. The missing heat, Trenberth and his fellow researchers concluded, is sequestered in the ocean below 700 metres (Balmaseda et al., 2013; Meehl et al., 2011). Two Dutch researchers, Caroline Katsman and Geert van Oldenborgh (2011), concur. Using an ensemble of climate model simulations, they report that during the period between

2003 and 2010, the heat loss is explained by increased radiation to space (45%) and increased deep-ocean warming (35%). In the coming years, they predict a resumption of an upward heating trend in the upper ocean.

Not all scientists agree with this interpretation. Judith Curry, a climate scientist at the Georgia Institute of Technology, who has long been critical of the climate-modelling establishment, questions this 'deep oceans as the hiding spot for the missing heat' explanation. In a series of posts on her blog, Climate Etc., Curry questions the quality of the 'reanalysis data' on which heat content measurements are based. She concludes,

> All in all, I don't see a very convincing case for deep ocean sequestration of heat. And even if the heat from surface heating of the ocean did make it into the deep ocean, presumably the only way for this to happen involves mixing (rather than adiabatic processes), so it is very difficult to imagine how this heat could reappear at the surface in light of the 2nd law of thermodynamics. (Curry, 2014)

Roger Pielke, Sr, an environmental scientist who has been following the global climate change debate for a long time, raises another type of concern. Pielke says that there is evidence of a strong positive linear trend in world ocean heat content since 1955, one third of which occurs in the 700–2,000-metre layer of the ocean. If indeed this is the case, then Pielke believes that it dismisses the value of using the annual average global surface temperature trend as the diagnostic to monitor global warming.[3]

The 'missing heat' debate offers both unprecedented opportunities and pitfalls for ocean scientists. If indeed deeper waters are heating, while surface waters are not, through what mechanism(s) is the heat migrating to the depths? Is it likely to head back up to the surface at some point? And what ecological damage (if any) could it wreak at the lower depths? These are questions that cannot be easily resolved solely through re-analysis of historical data by climate modellers. As Claire Parkinson (2010: 236) observes, 'No computer model fully mimics the entire climate system, and all modelers are aware that the models have limitations and that the projections from the models should not be assumed to predict precisely what the future will be.'

These limitations invite oceanographers to leverage their expertise and take 'ownership' of the 'missing heat' question. Commenting more broadly, atmospheric scientists Gerald North and Robert Duce (2002: 85) predict that the relationship between oceanography and the climate system will constitute 'a very active field of research', and one that will 'continue to be of great interest through much of the twenty-first century', especially in light of the observational and modelling difficulties involved.

Answers to the 'missing heat' controversy could be found in an unlikely place, the study of currents and wave activity on and in oceans. Researchers from Swinburne University of Technology's Centre for Ocean Engineering Science and Technology (Australia) discovered that large waves such as those that occur in tropical storms and cyclones can contribute in mixing a wider layer of the upper ocean with the cooler, deeper parts, exchanging heat and CO_2 with the atmosphere. This mixed layer, they report, is generally shallow and only deepens significantly as a consequence of the intensification of wave activity during tropical cyclones (Toffoli et al., 2012). Alexander Babanin, Director of the Centre and one of the study co-authors, observed that this points to the advantages of incorporating wave physics into climate models, 'Right now small-scale wave physics and large-scale climate modeling exist separately. To improve prediction, wave modeling should be incorporated in larger climate models [and used in other oceanographic disciplines like marine biology]' ('Climate models should include ocean waves', 2012).

In another research study (Adams et al., 2011), a group of scientists at the WHOI found that larva that colonize deep-sea vents appear to be swept away into the open ocean by strong deep-sea currents, only to travel to other vents hundreds of miles away. As the author of an article in *The Economist* observes, 'The idea that surface winds can influence deep-sea currents is surprising, and it suggests that the atmosphere's influence may extend far deeper into the oceans than previously thought' (*Economist*, 2011).

Oceanographers thus far have mostly remained out of the line of fire in the 'climate wars', but greater active participation in this debate would inevitably be accompanied by more controversy. It would also risk shifting the discursive spotlight from an expressly ecological understanding of deep oceans to a more physically oriented 'operational' approach that focuses on diagnostics, trends and indicators, and is reminiscent in some ways of Cold War marine science. In so doing, I suspect we are in danger of taking a backwards step. Just when a new frontier of scientific knowledge about underwater volcanoes, hydrothermal vents, ecological communities sustained by chemical energy and other deep-sea phenomena is opening up, we risk being engulfed in a new geopolitics of the deep that revolves around an escalating competition for oceanic territory resources and influence in the Arctic, the South China Sea and the Western Pacific Ocean.

Notes

Introduction

1 The 'deep ocean' or 'deep sea' is usually said to start at a depth of about 200 metres, the break point between the continental shelf and the continental slope. At its deepest point, the Mariana Trench in the west Pacific, the ocean drops to 11,000 metres below sea level, 25% deeper than Mount Everest is high (Roberts et al., 2005: 2).

2 See *http://www.tv.com/shows/sea-hunt/the-manganese-story -111440/*. The episode itself can be viewed at *https:// www.youtube.com/watch?v=TGTbnlJGgZU*.

3 The Alberta tar (oil) sands are massive deposits of bitumen that are turned into light oil through a process that extracts, crushes and melts millions of tons of gritty black sand. Environmentalists have charged that this process pollutes the Athabasca River, sends toxins into the air and drains the water table. Its alleged environmental health costs include unusually high levels of rare cancers. DiCaprio visited the tar sands in August 2014 for an environmental documentary on which he was working. In so doing, he joined a raft of other celebrity activists – James Cameron, Archbishop Desmond Tutu, Neil Young – who have travelled to the facility.

4 Cold seep ecosystems occur along the continental margin where cool, chemical-rich water oozes from the seabed. Unique forms of wildlife are supported here. There is

some similarity with hydrothermal vent communities, but for the most part each supports a different set of species (Gjerde, 2006: 15).

5 I am grateful to an anonymous reviewer for this insight and for pointing me to Stuart Elden's article 'Secure the Volume' (2013).

6 Seven years later, Steinberg seems to recognize this. Citing the Mansfield (2004) article, he writes, 'In the case of the ocean recent environmental changes such as declines in fish stocks, . . . must be placed within the context of broader societal dynamics such as the increased intensity of global economic exchanges and the rise of national development policies' (2008: 2085).

7 Note that there are other modes of thinking in contemporary international relations and political geography, most notably feminist and postcolonial theorizing, which might be relevant in understanding the geopolitics of oceans. As Joanne Sharp (2003: 66) observes, feminist and postcolonial writers recognize the social construction of boundaries (and therefore, presumably of oceanic 'frontiers'), but they also realize that these constructed boundaries can 'have real consequences in the lives of people the world over'.

Chapter 1 Oceanic Frontiers: Harvesting the Commons

1 Eminent contributors to this issue included former astronaut Buzz Aldrin and divers/authors Robert Ballard, Joe MacInnis and Sylvia Earle.

2 'Why is space exploration more important than deep sea exploration?' Posted by Chronos on 6 March 2004. Accessed at *http://boards.straightdope.com/sdmb/show thread.php?t=259574*.

3 Part 1 ('The Frozen World') and Part 2 ('The Roof of the World') were penned by other authors.

4 The first era, 'Geography Fabulous', involved extravagant speculation, as medieval cartographers created maps with pictures of strange pageants, trees and beasts 'drawn with amazing precision in the midst of theoretically conceived continents' (Driver, 2001: 3). The third, 'Geography Triumphant', marked the irreversible closure of the epoch of open spaces, much in the same way that the

closing of the American West spelled the end of the frontier.

5 A century later, the commercial importance of telecommunications cable would again emerge as a key factor in accounting for the support by Bell Labs for the Heezen–Tharp sea-floor mapping study, a project that provided crucial evidence in support of the theory of plate tectonics (see Chapter 3).

6 The Mid-Ocean Dynamics Experiment was an international initiative to measure the general circulation of the Atlantic Ocean. It was proposed by Henry Melson Stommel of MIT, who believed that the ocean was as chaotic as the atmosphere. The flow of the seas, he predicted, is dictated by colliding currents and swirling eddies that periodically produce strong storms. Stommel's theory was validated by a field experiment conducted from March to mid-July 1973. It involved six research vessels, two aircraft and dozens of scientists (see Knoss, 2013).

7 There are also 'white smoker' chimneys, which form from lower temperature fluids.

8 The Clarion–Clipperton Zone is an area of the seabed broadly comparable in size to Europe, located in the Eastern Central Pacific Ocean. It has been the subject of scientific investigations, mineral prospecting and exploration since the 1960s. Although a test-mining operation was conducted in the area in the early 1970s, no commercial mining has yet taken place (Lodge et al., 2014: 66, 72).

9 Sulphides grow at the rate of a foot or more a year (as compared to nodules, which add an inch in a million years) and are considered 'easier and cheaper to mine and inch for inch vastly more valuable' (Simon, 1984: 131).

10 According to Jack Barkenbus (1979: 12–14), commercial exploitation of polymetallic nodules is made up of five separate activities or components: the mining device (usually a dredge); the lifting method; the surface mining vessel; ore transport transferring nodules from the mining vessel to ore carriers; and processing (refining the ore and extracting the minerals).

11 The methane exists in solid form and is trapped by water molecules without binding to them.

12 Previously, on 13 July 2010, the *Jiaolong*, named after a mythical sea dragon and carrying a crew of three aquanauts, had successfully completed a dive to 3,759 metres, using a robotic arm to plant a Chinese flag on the seabed (Chase, 2010).

Chapter 2 Governing the Abyss: Sharing the Commons

1 A second proclamation, issued simultaneously, dealt with coastal fisheries in relation to the high seas. It declared that henceforth the United States would regulate fisheries in those areas of the high seas contiguous to its coasts, although there would be no restrictions on navigation. This 'provoked little adverse comment' (Glassner, 1990: 5).

2 As Gullion (1968: 5) points out, during this era there was, in fact, 'no single law of the sea but a body of codes, international agreements, unilateral declarations, precedents, and traditional practices that affect activities on or under the surface of the high seas'.

3 The cannon-shot rule can be traced to the Dutch legal scholar Hugo Grotius, who asserted in *De jure belli ac Pacis* ('On the Law of War and Peace') (1625) that a nation could claim sovereignty over the amount of coastal water that its naval forces could protect. In the early seventeenth century, this was defined as the length of a cannon shot (Buck, 1998: 80).

4 Note that I have chosen to abbreviate this as 'LOSC' rather than 'UNCLOS', in order to distinguish it from the conference leading up to the legislation.

5 '*Mare liberum*' is a chapter in a larger, if lesser known, work, *De jure praedae* ('Freedom of Seas') (Buck, 1998: 79).

6 According to Grotius, *mare liberum* did *not* apply to territorial waters, which were governed by the 'cannon-shot rule' (see n. 3 above).

7 In 1599, Elizabeth had protested to King Christian IV of Denmark about the seizure of English fishing and trading ships in the North Sea, and for the first time invoked the 'Law of Nations' in favour of the principle of open seas (Roots, 1986: 7).

8 Edward Wenk (1972: 260), a civil engineer and risk analyst who served as the first science adviser to the US

Congress, confides that Pardo told him that he developed his brief without first consulting other UN representatives, which may help account for its 'electrifying impact' at the General Assembly. On the General Assembly Agenda, the Maltese item was rather awkwardly entitled 'Declaration and Treaty Concerning the Reservation Exclusively for Peaceful Purposes of the Sea-Bed and of the Ocean Floor, Underlying the Seas Beyond the Limits of National Jurisdiction, and the Use of Their Resources in the Interests of Mankind'. In addition to mineral resources, Pardo's proposal included living resources of the sea, that is, flora and fauna.

9 The demands of the NIEO programme included more aid, technology transfer, debt alleviation, capital investment and representation in international institutions (Catley and Keliat, 1997: 180).

10 Between 1990 and 1994, the UN Secretary-General called 15 'informal consultation' meetings attended by up to 90 delegates (Freestone, 2007: 509).

11 The Conference was divided into three committees: Committee I dealt with the seabed; Committee II with territorial seas, straits, islands, archipelagoes, the high seas, economic zones, the continental shelf and access to the sea by landlocked nations; Committee III with ocean pollution, scientific research and technology transfer.

12 The Leverings confirm this, relating how Engo sabotaged a compromise on seabed mining acceptable to both Western industrialized nations and Third World diplomats that had been worked out between Pinto and Leigh Ratiner, the chief US negotiator (Levering and Levering, 1999: 64).

13 President Johnson's call for open access to the deep ocean was likely motivated less by global equity considerations and more by concern that the regime of open access be maintained for the benefit of US corporations planning to become active in seabed mining (Brown et al., 1977: 74). Edward Wenk (1972: 258) observes that the Defense Department, although it had not been consulted in advance, was privately pleased because Johnson's position was 'well aligned with its necessary concern for freedom of the seas, favoring minimal areas under national sovereignty that could inhibit naval operations'.

14 The Area is defined in the Convention as 'the seabed and ocean floor and subsoil thereof, beyond the limits of national jurisdiction' (LOSC, Article 1, para. 1).

15 One dramatic example of this can be found in Southern Europe, where the Atlantic jellyfish, introduced from North America through untreated ballast water from tanker ships, has proliferated, accounting for 95% of the biomass in the Black Sea – ten times the world's annual fish catch (Freestone, 2007: 535).

Chapter 3   Sovereignty Games: Claiming the Commons

1 According to Peter Nolan (2013), the largest concentration of Britain's overseas EEZs is in the South Atlantic with a total area of over 1.4 million square miles. When the nation went to war with Argentina in 1982, Prime Minister Margaret Thatcher was, he claims, well aware that the real value of the Falklands, South Georgia and the Sandwich Islands was in their EEZs.

2 The Lomonosov Ridge was named after a famous Russian scientist, Mikhail Lomonosov (1711–65), in the late 1940s. Among Lomonosov's many accomplishments, he is credited with discovering the atmosphere of the planet Venus.

3 Foreign policy analysts have detected a new 'Great Game' that is currently occurring in Central Asia. But, as Alexander Cooley (2012) argues, this differs from the earlier iteration, insofar as the influence of the superpowers (China, Russia and the United States) is more muted with the rise of a number of aggressive new regional players.

4 Expenditures at the Naval Research Laboratory from 1940 to 1945 grew from $1.7 million to $13.7 million. The flow of government funds into the private oceanographic institutions was equally impressive. For example, the budget of the WHOI 'rose so spectacularly that as of 1942 publication of the annual treasurer's report was suspended for fear of revealing "the magnitude, if not the nature of the investigations being undertaken at the request of the government"' (Schlee, 1973: 182).

5 In the ocean sciences, the ONR supported research in physical oceanography; biological/chemical oceanography; marine geology and geophysics; ocean acoustics; remote sensing and space; and marine meteorology,

among other programme areas (National Research Council, 1999: 24).

6 Notable among these was Ocean Mining Associates of Gloucester Point, Virginia, a joint venture of US Steel, the Sun Company (formerly Sun Oil) and Union Minière of Belgium (Helvarg, 2006: 15).

7 Evidently, Taiwan had initially failed to respond to the IGY invitation to join. However, at the last moment, the US State Department, alarmed by China's participation in the conference (it joined in 1955), decided to push the Chinese Nationalist government in Taiwan to apply for participation in the IGY (Wang and Zhang, 2010: 149).

8 Unlike the *Nautilus*, the *Skate* not only dived beneath but it also surfaced at the Pole.

9 The South China Sea encompasses a section of the Pacific Ocean stretching roughly from Singapore and the Straits of Malacca in the southwest to the Strait of Taiwan in the northeast (Hong, 2012: 5).

10 Partner universities in this project are the Virginia Tech College of Engineering, Providence College in Rhode Island, the University of California Los Angeles, the University of Texas at Dallas and Stanford University.

11 After the Chinese deep-sea submersible vehicle *Jiaolong* completed a 118-day voyage in the south-west Indian Ocean, China offered to partner with India on seabed exploration and oceanic research and development in the region. Chinese officials cited the high risks and costs of undertaking a mining project in the area (*mining -technology.com*, 2015).

12 The Lomonosov formation can either be defined as an ocean ridge, thereby situating it outside any type of state jurisdiction, or as a submarine elevation that is geologically connected to the continental shelf (as the Russians, Danes and Canadians have suggested), thus providing physical scientific evidence to be mustered in support of a LOSC claim (Dodds, 2008: 1, n. 3).

13 Today, Chilingarov is celebrated in Russia as a national hero and was appointed by President Putin as his Special Envoy for International Cooperation in the Arctic and Antarctic. Despite the international furore that erupted as a result of the flag-planting, Chilingarov seems to have remained sanguine about this incident, recalling in a 2012 interview with Canadian journalist Matthew Fisher

that he was head of the Canada–USSR Friendship Society in the Soviet era and has been a friend of film director and deep-sea diver James Cameron for quite some time (Fisher, 2012b).

14 The Svalbard Archipelago is a group of islands lying approximately midway between northern Norway and the North Pole. They have been called an 'Arctic Galapagos' because of their unique flora and fauna, but also contain abundant coal, oil and gas reserves (Singh and Saguirian, 1993: 57).

15 While both formulae stipulate that an extension is measured from the base of the continental slope, the Gardiner Line proposes that a claim can be established with reference to the depth/thickness of sedimentary rocks overlying the continental crust, while the Hedberg Line uses a distance formula starting from the foot of the continental shelf (Dodds, 2010a: 68).

16 In the 1980s, Malaysia attempted to apply the common heritage principle developed for seabed resources to Antarctica, and to supplant the treaty system with United Nations jurisdiction. This effort was stoutly resisted by the treaty powers, who modified the system somewhat by adding ten additional states, five of which were 'developing nations' in the capacity of 'Consultative Parties' (Glassner, 1990: 100, 104).

Chapter 4   Saving the Ocean: Protecting the Commons

1 It would be fascinating to know what Friedmann would have to say about contemporary developments. Tragically, however, a little more than a year after his book was published, he was fatally stabbed in a robbery attempt while strolling in the Morningside Heights neighbourhood near his Columbia University office.

2 It is estimated that the average pH of ocean surface waters since the beginning of the Industrial Revolution has decreased by about 0.1 unit and will drop by an additional 0.2–0.3 units by the end of the twenty-first century (National Research Council, 2010: 1).

3 I have borrowed this phrase from Thomas and Bowers (2012: Chap. 12).

4 The other three basic ocean science disciplines are: marine geology and geophysics; chemical oceanography; and

physical oceanography (National Research Council, 1999: 27–8).

5 The equilibrium state is defined here as one in which 'population and capital are essentially stable, with the forces tending to increase or decrease them in a carefully controlled balance' (Meadows et al., 1972: 171).

6 This is considerably fewer than the number of seamounts that would have been included if the recommendation to extend the reserve to 200 nautical miles surrounding each of the seven islands and atolls had been followed (Eilperin, 2014). In the event, the 200-nautical-mile offshore protection was applied to three areas – Wake Island, Johnson Atoll and Jarvis Island – while the remaining four – Howland and Baker islands, Kingman Reef and Palmyra Atoll – kept their 50-nautical-mile offshore protection.

7 In 1965, Britain split the Chagos Archipelago from Mauritius to form the British Indian Ocean Territory, primarily to allow the UK to lease Diego Garcia to the United States for use as an airbase suitable for heavy bombers. The British Indian Ocean Territory consists of a group of widely dispersed islands with a total land area of just 23 square miles, but an EEZ of around 247,000 square miles (Nolan, 2013).

Conclusion: Global Climate Change and the Future of Deep Oceans

1 *http://www.pices.int/meetings/international_symposia/2015/2015-Climate-Change/scope.aspx*.

2 POGO originated in March 1999, when the directors of the Scripps Institution of Oceanography, the WHOI and the Southampton Oceanography Centre in the UK convened a planning meeting in the headquarters of the United Nations Intergovernmental Oceanographic Commission (IOC). Scripps hosted the first formal meeting of POGO in early December 1999. The organization now includes 37 members in 21 countries. In addition to the three founding members, POGO currently includes such well-known research centres as the British Antarctic Survey, CSIRO Marine and Atmospheric Research (Australia), GEOMAR (Germany) and the NOAA (US).

3 One reviewer pointed out that I should not have inserted the Curry blog and Pielke Sr comments in this chapter, insofar as this appears to equate them with peer-reviewed research, as if both were equally compelling. My point is that, not unexpectedly given the stakes, the 'missing heat debate' has already begun to mobilize the 'two tribes' in the climate change wars. In this conflict, challengers have frequently resorted to publishing in online venues because they have routinely been kept out of the mainstream journals controlled by mainstream climate modellers. Judith Curry, in particular, has been outspoken on the issue of a closed world of climate science where 'the climate research establishment appealed to its own authority' (Pearce, 2010: 226–7).

References

AAAS (American Association for the Advancement of Science) (2009) Deep sea floor mining is subject of international colloquium. *EurekAlert*, 26 March. Accessed at *http://www.eurek alert.org/pub_releases/2009-03/whoi-dsf032609.php*.

Abadia, R., Day, B., Baron, N., et al. (2004) Defying ocean's end through the power of communications. In L. K. Glover and S. A. Earle (eds) *Defying Ocean's End: An Agenda for Action*. Island Press, Washington, DC, pp. 183–96.

Adams, D. K., McGillicuddy, D. J., Jr, Zamudio, L., et al. (2011) Surface-generated mesoscale eddies transport deep-sea products from hydrothermal vents. *Science* 332, 580–3.

Adler-Nissen, R. and Gammeltoft-Hansen, T. (eds) (2008a) *Sovereignty Games: Instrumentalizing State Sovereignty in Europe and Beyond*. Palgrave Macmillan, New York.

Adler-Nissen, R. and Gammeltoft-Hansen, T. (2008b) Epilogue: three layers of a contested concept. In R. Adler-Nissen and T. Gammeltoft-Hansen (eds) *Sovereignty Games: Instrumentalizing State Sovereignty in Europe and Beyond*. Palgrave Macmillan, New York, pp. 197–209.

Agardy, T. (2010) *Ocean Zoning: Making Marine Management More Effective*. Earthscan, London and Washington, DC.

Albion, R. G. (1965) Introduction. In R. G. Albion (ed.) *Exploration and Discovery*. Macmillan, New York and London.

Allen, B. (ed.) (2002) *The Faber Book of Exploration: An Anthology of Worlds Revealed by Explorers Through the Ages*. Faber and Faber, London.

Allen, S. (1996) National interest and collective security in the ocean regime. In E. M. Borgese, N. Ginsburg and J. R. Morgan (eds) *Ocean Yearbook 12*. University of Chicago Press, Chicago and London, pp. 19–31.

Amer, R. (2014) China, Vietnam and the South China Sea: disputes and dispute management. *Ocean Development & International Law* 45(1), 17–40.

Angley, N. (2013) Robotic jellyfish could be undersea spy. *CNN Tech*, 8 May. Accessed at *http://edition.cnn.com/2013/05/08/tech/innovation/robotic-jellyfish/*.

Aplin, G., Beggs, P., Brierley, G., et al. (1995) *Global Environmental Crises: An Australian Perspective*. Oxford University Press, Oxford.

Armeni, C. (2013) Carbon dioxide storage in the sub-seabed and sustainable development: please mind the gap. In A. Chircop, S. Coffen-Smout and M. McConnell (eds) *Ocean Yearbook 27*. University of Chicago Press, Chicago and London, pp. 1–27.

Arnold, D. (1983) *The Age of Discovery 1400–1600*. Methuen, London and New York.

Ascencio, A. and Bliss, M. (2003) Conserving the biodiversity of the high seas and deep oceans: institutional gaps in the international system. Contribution to the Cairns High Seas Biodiversity Workshop, 16–20 June.

Asimov, I. (1964) Visit to the World's Fair of 2014. *New York Times*, 16 August. Accessed at *http://www.nytimes.com/books/97/03/23/lifetimes/asi-v-fair.html*.

Asimov, I. (1987) *Frontiers: New Discoveries about Man and His Planet, Outer Space and the Universe*. E. P. Dutton, New York.

Baker, B. (2012) Uncommon heritage: Elisabeth Mann Borgese, *Pacem in Maribus*, the International Ocean Institute and Preparations for UNCLOS III. In A. Chircop, S. Coffen-Smout and M. McConnell (eds) *Ocean Yearbook 26*. University of Chicago Press, Chicago and London, pp. 11–34.

Baker, M. C., Bett, B. J., Billett, D. S. M. and Rogers, A. D. (2001) *The Status of Natural Resources on the High Seas: Part I – An Environmental Perspective*. WWF–World Wide Fund for Nature, Gland, Switzerland, pp. 1–68.

Balmaseda, M. A., Trenberth, K. E. and Källén, E. (2013) Distinctive climate signals in reanalysis of global ocean heat content. *Geophysical Research Letters* 40(9), 1754–9. Accessed at *http://www.cgd.ucar.edu/cas/Trenberth/website-archive/trenberth.papers-moved/Balmaseda_Trenberth_Kallen_grl_13.pdf*.

Barkenbus, J. N. (1979) *Deep Seabed Resources: Politics and Technology*. Free Press, New York.

Bateman, S. (2009) *Clashes at Sea: When Chinese Vessels Harass US Ships*. 27 RSIS Commentaries 2 (S. Rajaratnam School of International Studies, NTU, Singapore), 12 March.

BBC News (2014) Sweden could use force against suspected foreign sub. 22 October. Accessed at *http://www.bbc.com/news/world-europe-29721461*.

Bederman, D. J. (2008) *Globalization and International Law*. Palgrave Macmillan, New York.

Beesley, J. A. (2004) Grotius and the New Law. In A. Chircop and M. McConnell (eds) *Ocean Yearbook 18*. University of Chicago Press, Chicago and London, pp. 98–116.

Belanger, D. O. (2010) The International Geophysical Year in Antarctica: a triumph of 'apolitical' science, politics and peace. In R. D. Launius, J. R. Fleming and D. H. DeVorkin (eds) *Globalizing Polar Science: Considering the International Polar and Geophysical Years*. Palgrave Macmillan, New York, pp. 265–78.

Bell, M. M. (2003) Review of P. E. Steinberg, *The Social Construction of the Ocean* (2001). *American Journal of Sociology* 109(1), 217–18.

Bolster, J. W. (2006) Opportunities for marine environmental history. *Environmental History* 11(3), 567–97.

Borenstein, S. (2012) Digging deep for clues to life in outer space. *Toronto Star*, 10 February, p. A13.

Borgerson, S. G. (2008) Arctic meltdown: the economic and security implications of global warming. *Foreign Affairs* 87(2), 63–77.

Borgese, E. M. (1998) *The Oceanic Circle: Governing the Seas as a Global Resource*. United Nations University Press, Tokyo.

Boulding, K. E. (1966) The economics of the coming spaceship earth. In H. Jarrett (ed.) *Environmental Quality in a Growing Economy*. Johns Hopkins University Press/Resources for the Future, Baltimore, MD, pp. 3–14.

Bowcott, O. (2007) The new British empire? UK plans to annex south Atlantic. *Guardian*, 22 September. Accessed at *http://www.theguardian.com/uk/2007/sep/22/oil.politics*.

Brekke, H. (1997) Defining and recognizing the outer limits of the continental shelf in the polar regions. In W. J. Broad (ed.) *The Universe Below: Discovering the Secrets of the Deep Sea*. Simon & Schuster, New York, pp. 38–54.

Bridge, G. and Le Billon, P. (2013) *Oil*. Polity, Cambridge.

Broad, W. J. (1997) *The Universe Below: Discovering the Secrets of the Deep Sea*. Simon & Schuster: New York.

Brown, E. D. (1986) The legal regime and the UN Convention on the Law of the Sea. In *Advances in Underwater Technology, Ocean Science and Offshore Engineering, Volume 8: Exclusive*

Economic Zones: Resources, Opportunities and the Legal Regime. Graham and Trotman Ltd, London, pp. 15–35.

Brown, S., Cornell, N. W., Fabian, L. L. and Weiss, E. B. (1977) *Regimes for the Ocean, Outer Space and Weather*. Brookings Institution, Washington, DC.

Buck, S. J. (1998) *The Global Commons: An Introduction*. Island Press, Washington, DC.

Buckley, C. (2010) Marine Life Census reveals previously unknown sea creatures. *UConn Today*, 19 April. Accessed at *http://today. uconn.edu/blog/2010/04/marine-life-census-reveals-previously-unknown-sea-creatures/*.

Burstyn, H. L. (2001) Big science in Victorian Britain: the *Challenger* expedition (1872–6) and its Report (1881–95). In M. Deacon, T. Rice and C. Summerhayes (eds) *Understanding the Oceans: A Century of Ocean Exploration*. Routledge, London and New York, pp. 49–55.

Cameron, J. (2004) The drive to discover. *Wired*, December, pp. 188–91.

Caron, D. A. (1992) An introduction to biological oceanography. *Oceanus* 35(3), 10–17.

Catley, B. and Keliat, M. (1997) *Spratlys: The Dispute in the South China Sea*. Ashgate, Aldershot.

Chase, M. S. (2010) Capabilities and implications of China's *Jiaolong* submersible. *China Brief* (Jamestown Foundation) 10(23), 9 November. Accessed at *http://www.jamestown.org/programs/ chinabrief/single/?tx_ttnews%5Btt_news%5D=37197&cHash= 19169e46c7*.

China Daily (2013) Submersible taps mineral deposits in S. China Sea. 5 August. Accessed at *http://usa.chinadaily.com.cn/ china/2013-07/05/content_16730734.htm*.

Cicantell, P. S. (1999) It's all about power: the political economy and ecology of redefining the Brazilian Amazon. *The Sociological Quarterly* 40(2), 293–315.

Cicin-Sain, B. and Knecht, R. W. (2000) *The Future of US Ocean Policy: Choices for the New Century*. Island Press, Washington, DC.

Clarke, A. C. (1960) *The Challenge of the Sea* (Introduction by W. von Braun). Dell, New York.

Cleave, P. (1989) *The Sovereignty Game: Power, Knowledge and Reading the Treaty*. Victoria University Press, Wellington.

Cleveland, C. J. (1995) Biophysical economics: historical perspectives and current research trends. In R. Krishnan, J. M. Harris and N. R. Goodwin (eds) *A Survey of Ecological Economics*. Island Press, Washington, DC, pp. 29–32. (Excerpted from *Ecological Modelling* 38 [September 1987], 47–73.)

Cocco, E. (2013) Theoretical implications of maritime sociology. *Annuals of Marine Sociology* (*Roczniki Socjologii Morskiej*) XXII, 5–18. Accessed at *http://www.ceeol.com/aspx/issuedetails.aspx?issueid=5d136774-b3e1-4bd3-b496-babdad060585*.

Coffey, T. (2002) Challenges and opportunities in naval oceanography in the post-Cold War world. In K. R. Benson and P. R. Rehbock (eds) *Oceanographic History: The Pacific and Beyond*. University of Washington Press, Seattle, pp. 343–50.

Conrad, J. (1926) Geography and its explorers. In R. Curle (ed.) *Last Essays*. Blackwell, Oxford, pp. 1–31.

Cooley, A. (2012) The new Great Game in Central Asia. *Foreign Affairs*, 7 August. Accessed at *http://www.foreignaffairs.com/articles/137813/alexander-cooley/the-new-great-game-in-central-asia*.

Cooley, S. R. and Mathis, J. T. (2013) Addressing ocean acidification as part of sustainable ocean development. In A. Chircop, S. Coffen-Smout and M. McConnell (eds) *Ocean Yearbook 27*. University of Chicago Press, Chicago and London, pp. 29–47.

Corliss, J., Dymond, M., Gordon, L. I., et al. (1979) Submarine thermal springs on the Galapagos Rift. *Science* 203, 1073–83.

Costanza, R., Andrade, F., Antunes, P., et al. (1999) Ecological economics and sustainable governance of the oceans. *Ecological Economics* 31, 171–87.

Coughlin, C. (2014) Sub hunt dredges Cold War tensions. *National Post* (Canada), 21 October, p. A3.

Cousteau, J. (1974) *The Ocean World of Jacques Cousteau: Riches of the Sea*. The World Publishing Company, New York.

Cowen, R. C. (1960) *Frontiers of the Sea: The Story of Oceanographic Exploration* (Introduction by R. Revelle). Doubleday & Company, Inc., Garden City, NY.

Cronan, D. S. (1990) Overview of mineral resources in the UK. In D. A. Ardus and M. A. Champ (eds) *Ocean Resources: Volume 1: Assessment and Utilisation*. Kluwer Academic Publishers, Dordrecht, The Netherlands, pp. 105–11.

Curry, J. (2014) Ocean heat content uncertainties. *Climate Etc.* (blog), 21 January. Accessed at *http://judithcurry.com/2014/01/21/ocean-heat-content-uncertainties/*.

Daly, H. E. (1971) Toward a stationary-state economy. In J. Harte and R. Socolow (eds) *The Patient Earth*. Holt, Rinehart and Winston, New York, pp. 226–44.

Daly, H. E. (1973) *Toward a Steady-State Economy*. W. H. Freeman, San Francisco.

Daly, H. E. (1990) Toward some operational principles of sustainable development. *Ecological Economics* 2, 1–6.

Day, D. A. (2008) The spacecraft and the submarine. *The Space Review* 2, September. Accessed at *http://www.thespacereview.com/article/1202/1*.

Deacon, M. and Summerhayes, C. (2001) Introduction. In M. Deacon, T. Rice and C. Summerhayes (eds) *Understanding the Oceans: A Century of Ocean Exploration*. Routledge, London and New York, pp. 1–23.

Deleuze, G. and Guattari, F. (1987) *A Thousand Plateaus: Capitalism and Schizophrenia*. Translated by B. Massumi. University of Minnesota Press, Minneapolis.

DeLong, E. F. and Ward, D. M. (1992) Biological oceanography from a molecular perspective. *Oceanus* 35(3), 47–54.

Den Tandt, M. (2014) PM's polar pastimes need spark. *National Post* (Canada), 20 August, p. A5.

DeSombre, E. R. and Barkin, S. (2011) *Fish*. Polity, Cambridge.

Dittmer, J., Moisio, S., Ingram, A. and Dodds, K. (2011) Have you heard the one about the disappearing ice? Recasting Arctic geopolitics. *Political Geography* 30(4), 202–14.

Dixon, A. D. and Monk, A. H. B. (2014) Frontier finance. *Annals of the Association of American Geographers* 104(4), 852–68.

Dodds, K. (2007) *Geopolitics: A Very Short Introduction*. Oxford University Press, Oxford.

Dodds, K. (2008) Icy geopolitics. *Environment and Planning D: Society and Space* 26, 1–6.

Dodds, K. (2010a) Flag planting and finger pointing: the Law of the Sea, the Arctic and the political geographies of the outer continental shelf. *Political Geography* 29, 63–73.

Dodds, K. (2010b) Assault on the unknown: geopolitics, Antarctic science and the International Geophysical Year (1957–8). In S. Naylor and J. R. Ryan (eds) *New Spaces of Exploration: Geographies of Discovery in the Twentieth Century*. I. B. Tauris, London, pp. 148–72.

Dodds, K. (2010c) Governing Antarctica: contemporary challenges and the enduring legacy of the 1959 Antarctic Treaty. *Global Policy* 1(1), 108–15.

Dodds, K. (2013) Introduction: geopolitics and its critics. In K. Dodds, M. Kuus and J. Sharp (eds) *The Ashgate Research Companion to Critical Geopolitics*. Ashgate, Farnham, Surrey, pp. 1–17.

Doel, R. E., Levin, T. J. and Marker, M. K. (2006) Extending modern cartography to the ocean depths: military patronage, Cold War priorities and the Heezen–Tharp mapping project, 1952–1959. *Journal of Historical Geography* 32(3), 605–26.

Driscoll, N. W., Weissel, J. W. and Goff, J. A. (2000) Potential for large-scale submarine slope failure and tsunami generation along the US mid-Atlantic coast. *Geology* 28, 407–10.

Driver, F. (2001) *Geography Militant: Cultures of Exploration and Empire*. Blackwell, Oxford and Malden, MA.

Dryzek, J. S. (2005) *The Politics of the Earth: Environmental Discourses*. Oxford University Press, New York.

Duff, J. (2014) Review of M. H. Nordquist et al., *The Law of the Sea Convention: US Accession and Globalization* (Martinus Nijhoff Publishers, Leiden, 2012). In A. Chircop, S. Coffen-Smout and M. McConnell (eds) *Ocean Yearbook 28*. University of Chicago Press, Chicago and London, pp. 751–8.

Duvall, R. and Havercroft, J. (2009) Critical astropolitics: the geopolitics of space control and the transformation of state sovereignty. In N. Bormann and M. Sheehan (eds) *Securing Outer Space*. Routledge, London and New York, pp. 42–58.

Dyer, G. (2012) Race for Arctic mostly rhetoric. *Winnipeg Free Press*, 4 August, p. J1.

Economist (2011) Deep sea vents: ocean floor migration. 28 April.

Egede, E. and Sutch, P. (2013) *The Politics of International Law and International Justice*. Edinburgh University Press, Edinburgh.

Eilperin, J. (2014) Why is Obama protecting a place you've never heard of? We explain. *Washington Post*, 17 June. Accessed at *http://www.washingtonpost.com/blogs/the-fix/wp/2014/06/17/why-is-obama-protecting-a-place-youve-never-heard-of-we-explain*.

Elden, S. (2013) Secure the volume: vertical geopolitics and the depth of power. *Political Geography* 34, 35–51.

Ellis, R. (1996) *Deep Atlantic: Life, Death, and Exploration in the Abyss*. Alfred A. Knopf, New York.

Embley, R. W. (2007) The ocean floor. In *Hidden Depths: Atlas of the Ocean*. HarperCollins, New York, pp. 20–9.

Emery, K. O. (1979) Potential for deep-ocean petroleum. In Royal Swedish Academy of Sciences, *The Deep Sea – Ecology and Exploitation*. Lund, Sweden (*Ambio* Special Report, No. 6), pp. 87–92.

Endfield, G. H. (2009) Environmental history. In N. Castree, D. Demeritt, D. Liverman and B. Rhoads (eds) *A Companion to Environmental Geography*. Wiley-Blackwell, Oxford and Malden, MA, pp. 223–37.

Farquharson, A. (2013) Aquatopia: the imaginary of the ocean deep. In A. Farquharson and M. Clark (eds) *Aquatopia*. Nottingham Contemporary and Tate St Ives, London, pp. 6–11.

Fatouros, A. (2006) Concluding remarks. In A. Strati, M. Gavouneli and N. Skourtos (eds) *Unresolved Issues and New Challenges to* the Law of the Sea: Time Before and Time After. Martinus Nijhoff Publishers, Leiden, pp. 271–4.

Fisher, M. (2012a) Hands across the polar ice cap. National Post (Canada), 5 October, p. A2.

Fisher, M. (2012b) Arctic will make Canada rich: scientist. National Post (Canada), 9 October, p. A4.

Flint, C. (2011) Introduction to Geopolitics, 2nd edn. Routledge, New York and London.

Foucault, M. (1980) Power/Knowledge: Selected Interviews and Other Writings 1972–1977. Pantheon Books, New York.

Fox, D. (2014) Antarctica and the Arctic: a polar primer for the new Great Game. The Christian Science Monitor, 12 January. Accessed at http://www.csmonitor.com/World/Global-Issues/2014/0112/Antarctica-and-the-Arctic-A-polar-primer-for-the-new-great-game.

Fox, R. L. (2015) Britain's underwater gardens. Financial Times, 3 May, Weekend, House and Home section, pp. 1, 7.

Freestone, D. (2007) A decade of the Law of the Sea Convention: is it a success? George Washington International Law Review 39(3), 499–542.

Friedmann, W. (1971) The Future of the Oceans. George Braziller, New York.

Fujita, R. (2003) Heal the Ocean: Solutions for Saving our Oceans. New Society Publishers, Gabriola Island, BC.

Fukui, H. (1984) How Japan handled UNCLOS issues. Does Japan have an ocean policy? In R. L. Friedheim, G. O. Totten, H. Fukui et al. (eds) Japan and the New Ocean Regime. Westview Press, Boulder, CO, pp. 21–74.

Gammeltoft-Hansen, T. and Adler-Nissen, R. (2008) An introduction to sovereignty games. In R. Adler-Nissen and T. Gammeltoft-Hansen (eds) Sovereignty Games: Instrumentalizing State Sovereignty in Europe and Beyond. Palgrave Macmillan, New York, pp. 1–17.

Gattuso, J.-P. and Hansson, L. (2011) Ocean Acidification. Oxford University Press, Oxford.

Gau, M. S. (2014) The Sino-Philippine arbitration of the South China Sea nine-dash dispute: applying the rule of default of appearance. In A. Chircop, S. Coffen-Smout and M. McConnell (eds) Ocean Yearbook 28. University of Chicago Press, Chicago and London, pp. 81–133.

Gavouneli, M. (2006) From uniformity to fragmentation: the ability of the UN Convention on the Law of the Sea to accommodate new uses and challenges. In A. Strati, M. Gavouneli and N. Skourtos (eds) Unresolved Issues and New Challenges to the

Law of the Sea: Time Before and Time After. Martinus Nijhoff Publishers, Leiden, pp. 205–34.

Gavouneli, M. (2007) *Functional Jurisdiction in the Law of the Sea*. Martinus Nijhoff Publishers, Leiden and Boston.

Georgescu-Roegen, N. (1971) *The Entropy Law and the Economic Process*. Harvard University Press, Cambridge, MA.

Gibbons, M. and Spagni, D. A. (1986) The development of an integrated marine policy for the EEZ: the case of Japan. In *Advances in Underwater Technology, Ocean Science and Off-shore Engineering, Volume 8: Exclusive Economic Zones: Resources, Opportunities and the Legal Regime*. Graham and Trotman Ltd, London, pp. 129–41.

Gill, L. (2012) Murder at mining convention shocked Timmins 25 years ago. *Timmins Times*, 14 March. Accessed at *http://www.timminstimes.com/ArticleDisplay.aspx?e=3494150*.

Gillies, R. (2014) Lost ship from doomed Franklin expedition discovered in the Arctic. *Huffington Post*, 10 September. Accessed at *http://www.huffingtonpost.com/2014/09/10/lost-ship-franklin -expedition_n_5795154.html*.

Giraudo, P. (2014) Forget the South China Sea: China's Great Game in the Arctic draws near. *The National Interest* (US), 4 August. Accessed at *http://nationalinterest.org/blog/the-buzz/forget-the-south-china-sea-chinas-great-game-the-arctic-11013*.

Gjerde, K. M. (2006) *Ecosystems and Biodiversity in Deep Waters and High Seas*. UNEP Regional Seas Reports and Studies No. 178, UNEP/IUCN, Switzerland.

Glassner, M. (1990) *Neptune's Domain: A Political Geography of the Sea*. Unwin Hyman, Boston.

Global Ocean Refuge System [Marine Conservation Institute] (2014) President Obama announces plan to create the largest marine protected area in the world with help from Marine Conservation Institute. Accessed at *http://globaloceanrefuge. org/2014/06/17/president-obama/*.

Glowka, L. (1996) The deepest of ironies: genetic resources, marine scientific research, and the Area. In E. M. Borgese, N. Ginsburg and J. R. Morgan (eds) *Ocean Yearbook 12*. University of Chicago Press, Chicago and London, pp. 154–78.

Good, G. A. (2010) Sydney Chapman: dynamo behind the International Geophysical Year. In R. D. Launius, J. R. Fleming and D. H. DeVorkin (eds) *Globalizing Polar Science: Considering the International Polar and Geophysical Years*. Palgrave Macmillan, New York, pp. 177–203.

Griffin, P. (2009) The spaces between us: the gendered politics of outer space. In N. Bormann and S. Sheehan (eds) *Securing Outer Space*. Routledge, London and New York, pp. 59–75.

Grondin, D. (2009) The (power) politics of space: the US astro-political discourse on global dominance in the War on Terror. In N. Bormann and S. Sheehan (eds) *Securing Outer Space*. Routledge, London and New York, pp. 108–27.

Gross, E. (2010) Non-governmental international marine science organizations. In G. Holland and D. Pugh (eds) *Troubled Waters: Ocean Science and Governance*. Cambridge University Press, Cambridge, pp. 138–48.

Grumbine, R. E. (1992) *Ghost Bears: Exploring the Biodiversity Crisis*. Island Press, Washington, DC.

Guberlet, M. L. (1964) *Explorers of the Sea: Famous Oceanographic Expeditions*. The Ronald Press Company, New York.

Gullion, E. A. (1968) New horizons at sea. In E. A. Gullion (ed.) *Uses of the Sea*. Prentice Hall, Englewood Cliffs, NJ, pp. 1–16.

Guymer, T. H., Challenor, P. G. and Srokosz, M. A. (2001) Oceanography from space: past successes, future challenges. In M. Deacon, T. Rice and C. Summerhayes (eds) *Understanding the Oceans: A Century of Ocean Exploration*. Routledge, London and New York, pp. 193–211.

Hall, D. (2013) *Land*. Polity, Cambridge.

Hamblin, J. D. (2005) *Oceanographers and the Cold War: Disciples of Marine Science*. University of Washington Press, Seattle and London.

Hannigan, J. (2011) Social challenges: causes, explanations and solutions. In T. Fitzpatrick (ed.) *Understanding the Environment and Social Policy*. Policy Press, Bristol, pp. 41–60.

Hannigan, J. (2012) *Disasters without Borders: The International Politics of Natural Disasters*. Polity, Cambridge.

Hannigan, J. (2014) *Environmental Sociology*, 3rd edn. Routledge, London and New York.

Hardin, G. (1968) The tragedy of the commons. *Science* 162, 1243–8.

Hare, S. R. and Mantua, N. J. (2000) Empirical evidence for North Pacific regime shifts in 1977 and 1989. *Progress in Oceanography* 47, 103–45.

Harper, C. L. (2001) *Environment and Society: Human Perspectives on Environmental Issues*, 2nd edn. Pearson/Prentice Hall, Upper Saddle River, NJ.

Harrabin, R. (2014) Science chief warns on acid oceans. *BBC News*, 24 October. Accessed at *http://www.bbc.co.uk/news/science-environment-29746880*.

Harris, J. M. (1995a) Overview essay to Part II (Definition, scope and interdisciplinary issues). In R. Krishnan, J. M. Harris and N. R. Goodwin (eds) *A Survey of Ecological Economics*. Island Press, Washington, DC, pp. 49–54.

Harris, J. M. (1995b) Overview essay to Part III (Theoretical frameworks and techniques). In R. Krishnan, J. M. Harris and N. R. Goodwin (eds) *A Survey of Ecological Economics*. Island Press, Washington, DC, pp. 97–105.

Harris, R. (2008) The mystery of global warming's missing heat. *National Public Radio*, 19 March. Accessed at *http://www.npr. org/templates/story/story.php?storyId=88520025.*

Heininen, L. (2014) Northern geopolitics: actors, interests, and processes in the circumpolar Arctic. In R. C. Powell and K. Dodds (eds) *Polar Geopolitics? Knowledges, Resources and Legal Regimes*. Edward Elgar, Cheltenham, UK, pp. 241–58.

Heirtzler, J. R. and Grassle, J. F. (1976) Deep-sea research by manned submersibles. *Science* 194, 294–9.

Helvarg, D. (2006) [2001] *Blue Frontier: Dispatches from America's Ocean Wilderness*, 2nd edn. Sierra Club Books, San Francisco.

Henkin, L. (1968) Changing law for the changing seas. In E. A. Gullion (ed.) *Uses of the Sea*. Prentice Hall, Englewood Cliffs, NJ, pp. 69–97.

Herber, B. P. (2006) Bioprospecting in Antarctica: the search for a policy regime. *Polar Record* 42(221), 139–46.

HERMES [Hotspot Ecosystem Research on the Margin of European Seas] (2006) Critical governance, socioeconomic, management, and scientific issues for the deep sea: first meeting of the HERMES Science-Policy Panel Workshop Report, Brussels, 1 December.

Herzig, P. (2013) Mining the oceans: risks and opportunities. Presentation to the Department of Geology, University of Toronto, 26 March.

Higgins, A. (2014) A rare Arctic land sale stokes worry in Norway. *New York Times*, 28 September. Accessed at *http://www. nytimes.com/2014/09/28/world/europe/a-rare-arctic-land-sale-stirs-concerns-in-norway.html.*

Hilton, S. L. and van Minnen, C. A. (2004) Frontiers and boundaries in US history: an introduction. In C. A. van Minnen and S. L. Hilton (eds) *Frontiers and Boundaries in US History*. VU University Press, Amsterdam, pp. 1–26.

Hine, R. V. and Faragher, J. M. (2007) *Frontiers: A Short History of the American West*. Yale University Press, New Haven and London.

Hlebica, J. (2002) Oceanography in a changing world. *Explorations* 9(1), 22–9.

Hoare, P. (2013) *Homo aquaticus*: the half-known life. In A. Farquharson and M. Clark (eds) *Aquatopia*. Nottingham Contemporary and Tate St Ives, London, pp. 14–21.

Hochschild, A. (1999) *King Leopold's Ghost: A Story of Greed, Terror and Heroism in Colonial Africa*. Mariner Books (Houghton Mifflin), Boston and New York.

Homeland Security News Wire (2013a) Military systems hibernate on the sea floor, then woken up remotely. 15 January. Accessed at *http://www.homelandsecuritynewswire.com/dr2013 0115-military-systems-hibernate-on-the-sea-floor-then-woken-up-remotely.*

Homeland Security News Wire (2013b) Large robotic jellyfish to patrol the oceans. 3 April. Accessed at *http://www.homeland securitynewswire.com/dr20130402-large-robotic-jellyfish-to-patrol-the-oceans.*

Hong, N. (2012) *UNCLOS and Ocean Dispute: Law and Politics in the South China Sea*. Routledge, London and New York.

Hopper, T. (2014) A new cold war: Denmark gets aggressive: stakes huge on claim for Race for Arctic. *National Post* (Toronto), 15 December, pp. A1, A9.

Hough, P. (2013) *International Politics of the Arctic: Coming in from the Cold*. Routledge, London and New York.

Howard, B. C. (2014) US creates largest protected area in the world, 3× larger than California. *National Geographic Online*, 24 September. Accessed at *http://news.nationalgeographic.com/news/2014/09/140924-pacific-remote-islands-marine-monument-expansion-conservation/.*

Hsü, K. J. (1983) *The Mediterranean Was a Desert: A Voyage of the Glomar Challenger*. Princeton University Press, Princeton.

Hsu, K. J. (1992) *Challenger at Sea: A Ship that Revolutionized Earth Science*. Princeton University Press, Princeton.

Indian Defence Forum (2011) China announces plan to expand seabed mining in the Indian Ocean. *Indian Defence.com*, 17 September. Accessed at *indiandefence.com/threads/china-announces-plan-to-expand-seabed-mining-in-indian-ocean. 11167/.*

International Mining (2014) Seven new exploration licences for deep sea mining. *International Mining*. 25 July. Accessed at *im-mining.com/2014/07/25/seven-new-exploration-licenses-for-deep-sea-mining/.*

International Seabed Authority (2013) 19th Session. Accessed at *https://www.isa.org.jm/sessions/19th-session-2013.*

IODP (International Ocean Discovery Program) (2007) Glomar Challenger: drillship of the Deep Sea Drilling Project. 28 November. Accessed at *http://www-odp.tamu.edu/glomar.html.*

Jacques, P. (with Smith, Z. A.) (2003) *Ocean Politics: A Reference Handbook*. ABC-CLIO, Santa Barbara, CA.

Jayawardhana, R. (2011) *Strange New Worlds: The Search for Alien Planets and Life Beyond Our Solar System.* HarperCollins Publishers Ltd, Toronto.

Jayewardene, H. W. (2001) The Indian Ocean: lessons learned. In M. J. Valencia (ed.) *Maritime Regime Building: Lessons Learned and Their Relevance for Northeast Asia.* Martinus Nijhoff Publishers, The Hague, pp. 105–29.

Jennings, F. D. (2000) *The Role of NSF in Big Ocean Science: 1950–1980, 30 Years of Ocean Discovery.* National Science Foundation/National Academies Press, Washington, DC.

JOGMEC (Japan Oil, Gas and Metals National Corporation) (2014) Promoting the development of methane hydrates. Accessed at *http://www.jogmec.go.jp/english/oil/technology_015.html.*

Johnson, L. (1967) Remarks at the commissioning of the research ship *Oceanographer,* 13 July 1966. In *Public Papers of the Presidents of the United States: Lyndon B. Johnson, 1966,* Vol. 2. GPO, Washington, DC, p. 724.

Katsman, C. A. and van Oldenborgh, G. J. (2011) Tracing the upper ocean's 'missing heat'. *Geophysical Research Letters* 38(L14610). Accessed at *http://www.knmi.nl/publications/full texts/katsman_vanoldenborgh2011.pdf.*

Kemp, G. (1981) Geopolitics, remote frontiers and outer space. *Fletcher Forum* 5(1), 115. Accessed at *http://dl.tufts.edu/catalog/ tufts:UP149.001.00009.00008.*

Kennedy, D. (2014) Introduction: reinterpreting exploration. In *Reinterpreting Exploration: The West in the World.* Oxford University Press, Oxford, pp. 1–18.

Keyuan, Z. (2012a) China's U-shaped line in the South China Sea revisited. *Ocean Development & International Law* 43(1), 18–34.

Keyuan, Z. (2012b) China and the United Nations Convention on the Law of the Sea: recent developments and prospects. In A. Chircop, S. Coffen-Smout and M. McConnell (eds) *Ocean Yearbook 26.* University of Chicago Press, Chicago and London, pp. 161–79.

Knoss, T. (2013) Mapping the storms of the sea. *MIT Technology Review,* 20 February. Accessed at *http://www.technologyreview. com/article/510856/mapping-the-storms-of-the-sea/.*

Koranyi, B. (2012) Clinton to assert US claim in Arctic. *Toronto Star,* 1 June, p. A23.

Koven, P. (2014) Nautilus closer to undersea mining. *National Post* (Toronto), 26 June, p. FP7.

Kraska, J. (2011) *Maritime Power and the Law of the Sea: Expeditionary Operations in World Politics.* Oxford University Press, New York.

Kristof, L. (1959) The nature of frontiers and boundaries. *Annals of the Association of American Geographers* 49, 269–82.

Kroll, G. (2008) *America's Ocean Wilderness: A Cultural History of Twentieth-Century Exploration*. University of Kansas Press, Lawrence.

Laursen, F. (1982) Security versus access to resources: explaining a decade of US ocean policy. *World Politics* 34(2), 197–229.

Levering, R. B. (1997) Brokering the Law of the Sea Treaty: the Neptune Group. In J. Smith, C. Chatfield and R. Pagnucco (eds) *Transnational Social Movements and Global Politics*. Syracuse University Press, Syracuse, NY, pp. 225–39.

Levering, R. B. and Levering, M. L. (1999) *Citizen Action for Global Change: The Neptune Group and the Law of the Sea*. Syracuse University Press, Syracuse, NY.

Levitus, S. (1982) *Climatological Atlas of the World's Oceans*. NOAA Professional Paper No. 13. US Government Printing Office, Washington, DC.

Levitus, S., Antonov, J. I., Boyer, T. P., et al. (2012) World ocean heat content and thermosteric sea level change (0–2000 m), 1955–2010. *Geophysical Research Letters* 39(L10603). doi:10.1029/2012GL051106.

Lewis, M. (2012) Billionaires eye asteroid-mining plan. *Toronto Star*, 24 April, pp. A1–2.

Lieberman, S. and Yang, J. (2013) Rio + 20 and the oceans: past, present, and future. In A. Chircop, S. Coffen-Smout and M. McConnell (eds) *Ocean Yearbook 27*. University of Chicago Press, Chicago and London, pp. 67–87.

Littleboy, A. and Boughen, N. (2007) Exploring the social dimensions of an expansion to the seafloor exploration and mining industry in Australia: Synthesis Report. CSIRO Wealth from Oceans Flagship Report P2007/917, North Ryde, NSW.

Locker, R. (2014) Pentagon boosting its push for underwater drones. *USA Today*, 13 March. Accessed at *http://www.usatoday.com/story/nation/2014/03/13/pentagon-upward-falling-payloads/6371505/*.

Lodge, M., Johnson, D., Le Gurun, G., et al. (2014) Seabed mining: International Seabed Authority environmental management plan for the Clarion–Clipperton Zone. A partnership approach. *Marine Policy* 49, 66–72.

Loftas, T. (1972) *The Last Resource: Man's Exploitation of the Oceans*. Penguin, Harmondsworth, UK.

McConnaughey, J. (2012) Robotic fish are being developed by the Navy. *Huff Post Tech*, 22 December. Accessed at *http://www.huffingtonpost.com/2012/10/23/robotic-fish-navy_n_2004366.html*.

McConnell, M. L. (2011) Observations on the law applicable on the continental shelf and the exclusive economic zone. In A. Chircop, S. Coffen-Smout and M. McConnell (eds) *Ocean Yearbook 25*. University of Chicago Press, Chicago and London, pp. 221–47.

McFadden, R. (2015) The lady of the sharks. *Globe & Mail*, 3 March, p. S8.

McGowan, J. A. and Field, J. G. (2002) Ocean studies. In J. G. Field, G. Hempel and C. P. Summerhayes (eds) *Oceans 2020: Science Trends, and the Challenge of Sustainability*. Island Press, Washington, DC, pp. 9–45.

McKibben, B. (2007a) Foreword. In J. Cousteau and S. Schiefelbein, *The Human, the Orchid, and the Octopus: Exploring and Conserving Our Natural World*. Bloomsbury, New York, pp. ix–xi.

McKibben, B. (2007b) *Deep Economy: The Wealth of Communities and the Durable Future*. Henry Holt and Company, New York.

McLean, C. N. and Readel, A. M. (2007) Human interaction. In *Hidden Depths: Atlas of the Ocean*. HarperCollins, New York, pp. 174–211.

Madin, L. P., Grassle, F., Azam, F., et al. (2004) The unknown ocean. In L. K. Glover and S. A. Earle (eds) *Defying Ocean's End: An Agenda for Action*. Island Press, Washington, DC, pp. 213–36.

Mansfield, B. (2004) Neoliberalism in the oceans: 'rationalization', property rights, and the commons question. *Geoforum 35*, 313–26.

Marine Conservation Institute (2014) Scientists' letter supporting marine reserves. Accessed at *http://www.marine-conservation.org/marine-reserve-statement/*.

MaritimeSecurity.Asia (2011) China signs contract for Indian Ocean mining rights. 22 November. Accessed at *http://maritimesecurity.asia/free-2/sea-lines-of-communication/china-signs-contract-for-indian-ocean-mining-rights/*.

Marx, W. (1981) *The Oceans: Our Last Resource*. Sierra Club Books, San Francisco.

Mathiason, J. (2007) *Invisible Governance: International Secretariats in Global Politics*. Kumarian Press, Inc., Bloomfield, CT.

Meadows, D. H., Meadows, D. L. and Randers, J. (1992) *Beyond the Limits: Confronting Global Collapse and Envisioning a Sustainable Future*. McClelland & Stewart, Toronto.

Meadows, D. H., Meadows, D. L., Randers, J. and Behrens, W. W., III (1972) *The Limits to Growth: A Report of The Club of Rome's Project on the Predicament of Mankind*. Universe Books, New York.

Meehl, G. A., Arblaster, J. M., Fasullo, J. T., et al. (2011) Model-based evidence of deep-ocean heat uptake during surface-temperature hiatus (letter). *Nature Climate Change* 1, 360–4.

Mels, T. (2009) Analysing environmental discourses and representations. In N. Castree, D. Demeritt, D. Liverman and B. Rhoads (eds) *A Companion to Environmental Geography*. Wiley-Blackwell, Oxford and Malden, MA, pp. 385–99.

Mercille, J. (2013) Radical geopolitics. In K. Dodds, M. Kuus and J. Sharp (eds) *The Ashgate Research Companion to Critical Geopolitics*. Ashgate, Farnham, UK, pp. 129–46.

Metro (Toronto) (2010) Can oceans predict the future? 1 November, p. 14.

Miles, E. L. (1998) *Global Ocean Politics: The Decision Process at the Third United Nations Conference on the Law of the Sea 1973–1982*. Martinus Nijhoff Publishers, The Hague.

Miller, S. L. and Bada, J. L. (1988) Submarine hot springs and the origin of life. *Nature* 534, 609–11.

Milligan, B. (2014) Planning for offshore CO_2 storage: law and policy in the United Kingdom. *Marine Policy* 48, 162–71.

Mills, E. L. (1983) Problems of deep-sea biology: an historical perspective. In G. T. Rowe (ed.) *Deep-Sea Biology*, Volume 8 of *The Sea: Ideas and Observations on Progress in the Study of the Seas*. John Wiley & Sons, New York, pp. 1–79.

Milun, K. (2011) *The Political Uncommons: The Cross-Cultural Logic of the Global Commons*. Ashgate, Farnham, UK.

mining-technology.com (2015) China and India may partner for seabed mineral exploration in Indian Ocean. 11 May. Accessed at *http://www.mining-technology.com/news/newschina-and-india-may-partner-for-seabed-mineral-exploration-in-indian-ocean-4573567*.

Monroe, R. (2005) Burning questions abound over methane hydrates. *Explorations* 12(1), 5–13.

Morris, C. (2014) Swedish search for 'foreign sub' focuses on Ingaro Bay. *BBC News*, 21 October. Accessed at *http://www.bbc.com/news/world-europe-29706661*.

Müller, M. (2013) Text, discourse, affect and things. In K. Dodds, M. Kuus and J. Sharp (eds) *The Ashgate Research Companion to Critical Geopolitics*. Ashgate, Farnham, UK, pp. 49–68.

Nadeau, R. L. (2006) *The Environmental Endgame: Mainstream Economics, Ecological Disaster, and Human Survival*. Rutgers University Press, New Brunswick, NJ.

Nandon, S. (2005) Administering the mineral resources of the deep seabed. The British Institute of International and Comparative Law Symposium, London, 22–3 March.

National Research Council (1999) *Global Ocean Science: Toward an Integrated Approach*. The National Academies Press, Washington, DC.

National Research Council (2003) *Exploration of the Seas: Voyage into the Unknown*. The National Academies Press, Washington, DC.

National Research Council (2010) *Ocean Acidification: A National Strategy to Meet the Challenges of a Changing Ocean*. The National Academies Press, Washington, DC.

Nautilus Minerals (2013) *Planning for Profits: Report on Mining* 16(1), Spring, 18–21.

New York Times (2014) Mr Obama's Pacific Monument. 1 October. Accessed at *http://www.nytimes.com/2014/10/02/opinion/mr-obamas-pacific-monument.html?_r=0*.

Nolan, P. (2013) Imperial archipelagos: China, Western colonialism and the Law of the Sea. *New Left Review* 80, March–April, 77–95.

Norse, E. A. (2005) Ending the range wars on the last frontier: zoning the sea. In E. A. Norse and L. B. Crowder (eds) *Marine Conservation Biology: The Science of Maintaining the Sea's Biodiversity*. Island Press, Washington, DC, pp. 422–43.

North, G. R. and Duce, R. A. (2002) Climate change and the ocean. In J. G. Field, G. Hempel and C. P. Summerhayes (eds) *Oceans 2020: Science, Trends and the Challenge of Sustainability*. Island Press, Washington, DC, pp. 85–108.

Nye, J. (2004) *Soft Power: The Means to Success in World Politics*. Public Affairs, New York.

Opie, J. (1979) Frontier history in environmental perspective. In J. O. Steffen (ed.) *The American West: New Perspectives, New Dimensions*. University of Oklahoma Press, Norman, pp. 9–34.

Oral, N. (2006) Protection of vulnerable marine ecosystems in areas beyond national jurisdiction: can international law meet the challenge? In A. Strati, M. Gavouneli and N. Skourtos (eds) *Unresolved Issues and New Challenges to the Law of the Sea: Time Before and Time After*. Martinus Nijhoff Publishers, Leiden, pp. 85–108.

Oreskes, N. (2003) A context of motivation: US Navy oceanographic research and the discovery of sea-floor hydrothermal vents. *Social Studies of Science* 33(5), 697–742.

Pardo, A. (1968) Who will control the seabed? *Foreign Affairs*, October. Accessed at *http://www.foreignaffairs.com/author/arvid-pardo*.

Pardo, A. (1978) The evolving law of the sea: a critique of the informal composite negotiating text (1977). In E. M. Borgese and

N. Ginsburg (eds) *Ocean Yearbook 1*. University of Chicago Press, Chicago and London, pp. 9–37.

Paris, M. (2013) Arctic ownership race about more than Santa and science: Kris Kringle and scientists aside, claiming the North Pole is all about geopolitics. *CBC.ca*, 16 December. Accessed at *http://www.cbc.ca/news/politics/arctic-ownership-race-about-more-than-santa-and-science-1.2463446*.

Parkinson, C. L. (2010) *Coming Climate Crisis: Consider the Past, Beware the Big Fix*. Rowman & Littlefield, Lanham, MD.

Payoyo, P. B. (1997) *Cries of the Sea: World Inequality, Sustainable Development and the Common Heritage of Humanity*. Martinus Nijhoff Publishers, The Hague.

Pearce, F. (1994) Disturbing the science of the deep: whales could be deafened by low-frequency sound soon to be blasted across the world's oceans. The aim? To monitor global warming. *The Independent*, 8 October. Accessed at *http://www.independent.co.uk/arts-entertainment/science–disturbing-the-silence-of-the-deep-whales-could-be-deafened-by-lowfrequency-sound-soon-to-be-blasted-across-the-worlds-oceans-the-aim-to-monitor-global-warming-fred-pearce-on-a-marine-controversy-1436191.html*.

Pearce, F. (2010) *The Climate Files: The Battle for the Truth about Global Warming*. Guardian Books, London.

Pease, K. S. (2008) *International Organizations: Perspectives on Governance in the Twenty-First Century*, 3rd edn. Pearson Prentice Hall, Upper Saddle River, NJ.

Peccei, A. (1977) *The Human Quality*. Pergamon Press, Oxford.

Pedrozo, R. (2009) Close encounters at sea: the USNS Impeccable. *Naval War College Review* 63(3). Accessed at *http://www.globalsecurity.org/military/library/report/2009/ada519335.pdf*.

Perlez, J. (2012) China asserts sea claim with politics and ships. *New York Times*, 11 August. Accessed at *http://www.nytimes.com/2012/08/12/world/asia/beijing-reasserts-its-claims-in-south-china-sea.html*.

Pew Environment Group (2012) *Out of the Abyss: Transforming EU Rules to Protect the Deep Sea*. Pew Environment Group, Washington, DC, 26 January. Accessed at *http://www.pewtrusts.org/~/media/legacy/uploadedfiles/peg/publications/report/deepOutoftheAbyssFinalmdpdf.pdf*.

Portecovo, G. (ed.) (1986) *The New Order of the Oceans*. Columbia University Press, New York.

Powell, R. C. and Dodds, K. (2014) Polar geopolitics. In R. C. Powell and K. Dodds (eds) *Polar Geopolitics? Knowledges, Resources and Legal Regimes*. Edward Elgar, Cheltenham, UK, pp. 3–18.

Prager, E. J. (with Earle, S. A.) (2000) *The Oceans*. McGraw-Hill, New York.

Prescott-Steed, D. J. (2012) A new frontier for visual culture: thoughts on the production and consumption of digital deep-sea imagery. *Kinema: A Journal for Film and Audiovisual Culture*, Fall. Accessed at *http://www.kinema.uwaterloo.ca/article.php?id =521&feature*.

Proujan, C. (1973) [1971] Secrets of the sea. In *Earth's Last Frontiers: A History of Discovery and Exploration*. Aldus Books/ Jupiter Books, London, pp. 323–481.

Ramirez-Llodra, E., Tyler, P. A., Baker, M. C., et al. (2011) Man and the last great wilderness: human impact on the deep sea. *PLoS ONE* 6(8), 1–25. Accessed at *http://www.plosone.org/ article/info%3Adoi%2F10.1371%2Fjournal.pone.0022588*.

Reagan, R. (1983) Statement on United States Oceans Policy. 10 March. Accessed at *http://www.reagan.utexas.edu/archives/ speeches/1983/31083c.htm*.

Redclift, M. (2006) *Frontiers: Histories of Civil Society and Nature*. MIT Press, Cambridge, MA.

Revelle, R. (1960) Introduction. In R. C. Cowen, *Frontiers of the Sea: The Story of Oceanographic Exploration*. Doubleday & Company, Inc., Garden City, NY, pp. 9–12.

Roberts, C. (2012) *The Ocean of Life*. Viking, New York.

Roberts, S., Aguilar, R., Warrenchuk, J., et al. (2005) *Deep Sea Life: On the Edge of the Abyss*. Oceana. Accessed at *http://oceana. org/sites/default/files/reports/Deep_Sea_Life_ENG.pdf*.

Robinson, M. F. (2014) Science and exploration. In D. Kennedy (ed.) *Reinterpreting Exploration: The West in the World*. Oxford University Press, Oxford, pp. 21–37.

Rochester, J. M. (2006) *Between Peril and Promise: The Politics of International Law*. CQ Press, Washington, DC.

Rogers, P. (2000) *Losing Control: Global Security in the Twenty-First Century*. Pluto Press, London.

Roots, E. F. (1986) Exclusive economic zones – a brief sketch of historical development and current issues. In *Advances in Underwater Technology, Ocean Science and Offshore Engineering, Volume 8: Exclusive Economic Zones: Resources, Opportunities and the Legal Regime*. Graham and Trotman Ltd, London, pp. 5–13.

Rozwadowski, H. M. (2005) *Fathoming the Ocean: The Discovery and Exploration of the Deep Sea*. Harvard University Press, Cambridge, MA, and London.

Rozwadowski, H. M. (2012) Arthur C. Clarke and the limitations of the ocean as a frontier. *Environmental History* 17(3), 578–602.

Russell, D. (2010) *Who Rules the Waves? Piracy, Overfishing and Mining the Oceans*. Pluto Press, London.

Sachs, J. (2006) The new geopolitics. *Scientific American*, 6 May. Accessed at *http://www.scientificamerican.com/article/the-new-geopolitics/*.

Said, E. W. (1978) *Orientalism*. Penguin, London.

Sala, E., Morgan, L., Norse, E. and Friedlander, A. (2014) *Expansion of the US Pacific Remote Islands Marine National Monument: The Largest Ocean Legacy on Earth*. Report to the United States Government, 20 May. Accessed at *http://www.marineconservation.org/media/filer_public/filer_public/2014/06/17/primnm_expansion_report.pdf*.

Scharper, S. B. (2014) Obama's lasting ecological legacy may be under the sea. *Toronto Star*, 6 October, p. A15.

Schiefelbein, S. (2007) Introduction. In J. Cousteau and S. Schiefelbein, *The Human, the Orchid, and the Octopus: Exploring and Conserving Our Natural World*. Bloomsbury, New York, pp. 1–25.

Schlee, S. (1973) *The Edge of an Unfamiliar World: A History of Oceanography*. E. P. Dutton & Co., Inc., New York.

Schmidt, V. A. (2008) Discourse institutionalism: the explanatory power of ideas and discourse. *Annual Review of Political Science* 11, 303–26.

Scovazzi, T. (2013) Review of H. Tuerk, *Reflections on the Contemporary Law of the Sea*. In A. Chircop, S. Coffen-Smout and M. McConnell (eds) *Ocean Yearbook 27*. University of Chicago Press, Chicago and London, pp. 551–6.

Sharma, O. P. (2009) *The International Law of the Sea: India and the UN Convention of 1982*. Oxford University Press, New Delhi.

Sharp, J. S. (2003) Feminist and postcolonial engagements. In J. Agnew, K. Mitchell and G. Toal (Ó Tuathail) (eds) *A Companion to Political Geography*. Blackwell, Malden, MA, pp. 59–74.

Shukman, D. (2013a) UK Seabed Resources joins deep-ocean mineral-mining rush. *BBC News Science & Environment*, 14 March. Accessed at *http://www.bbc.com/news/science-environment-21774447*.

Shukman, D. (2013b) Deep sea mining 'gold rush' moves closer. *BBC News Science & Environment*, 17 May. Accessed at *http://www.bbc.com/news/science-environment-22546875?filter=EditorPicks*.

Shukman, D. (2014) Agreement reached on deep sea mining. *BBC News Science & Environment*, 25 April. Accessed at *http://www.bbc.com/news/science-environment-27158883?postId=119323146*.

Siegel, S. (1999) Is spreading sonar smart science or overkill? *CNN. com*, 2 July. Accessed at *http://www.cnn.com/NATURE/9907/02/ sea.noise.part3/*.

Simon, A. W. (1984) *Neptune's Revenge: The Ocean of Tomorrow*. Franklin Watts, New York.

Singh, E. C. and Saguirian, A. A. (1993) The Svalbard Archipelago: the role of surrogate negotiators. In O. R. Young and G. Osherenko (eds) *Polar Politics: Creating International Environmental Regimes*. Cornell University Press, Ithaca, NY, pp. 56–95.

Slotkin, R. (1992) *Gunfighter Nation: The Myth of the Frontier in Twentieth-Century America*. University of Oklahoma Press, Norman.

Snyder, J. (2014) Wide swaths of Pacific to get shield in Obama plan. *Bloomberg.com*, 17 June. Accessed at *http://www.bloomberg. com/news/articles/2014-06-17/wide-swaths-of-pacific-to-get-shield-in-obama-plan*.

Soares, M. (Chairman) (1998) *The Ocean . . . Our Future: The Report of the Independent World Commission on the Oceans*. Cambridge University Press, Cambridge.

Stanek, B. (2014) Leonardo DiCaprio pledges to help save world's oceans. *Time*, 17 June. Accessed at *http://time.com/2890285/ leonardo-dicaprio-state-department-ocean-conservation/*.

Steinberg, P. E. (1999) Navigating the multiple horizons: toward a geography of ocean-space. *Professional Geographer* 51(3), 366–75.

Steinberg, P. E. (2001) *The Social Construction of the Ocean*. Cambridge University Press, Cambridge.

Steinberg, P. E. (2008) It's so easy being green: overuse, underexposure and the marine environmental consensus. *Geography Compass* 2(6), 2080–96.

Steinberg, P. E. (2014) Maintaining hegemony at a distance: ambivalence in US Arctic policy. In R.C. Powell and K. Dodds (eds) *Polar Geopolitics? Knowledges, Resources and Legal Regimes*. Edward Elgar, Cheltenham, UK, pp. 113–30.

Stuart, J. (2009) Unbundling sovereignty, territory, and the state in outer space: two approaches. In N. Borman and M. Sheehan (eds) *Securing Outer Space*. Routledge, New York, pp. 8–23.

Suess, E., Bohrmann, G., Greinhert, J. and Lausch, E. (2007) Flammable ice. In *Oceans: A Scientific American Reader*. University of Chicago Press, Chicago and London, pp. 263–72.

Swinburne University of Technology (2012) Climate models should include ocean waves. Media release, Swinburne University of Technology, 14 June. Accessed at *http://www.swinburne.edu.au/ chancellery/mediacentre/media-centre/news/2012/06/climate-models-should-include-ocean-waves*.

Thomas, D. N. and Bowers, D. G. (2012) *Introducing Oceanography*. Dunedin Academic Press, Edinburgh.

Tinbergen, J. (ed.) (1977) *Reshaping the International Order (RIO): A Report to the Club of Rome*. Hutchinson, London.

Tivey, M. K. (1991/2) Hydrothermal vent systems. *Oceanus* 34(4), 68–74.

Toffler, A. (1970) *Future Shock*. Random House, New York.

Toffoli, A., McConochie, J., Ghantous, M., Loffredo, L. and Babanin, A. V. (2012) The effect of wave-induced turbulence on the ocean mixed layer during tropical cyclones: field observations on the Australian North-West Shelf. *Journal of Geophysical Research: Oceans (1978–2012)* 117(C11). doi:10.1029/2011JC007780.

Tuerk, H. (2012) *Reflections on the Contemporary Law of the Sea*. Martinus Nijhoff Publishers, Leiden and Boston.

Turner, F. J. (1893) The significance of the frontier in American history. *The Annual Report of the American Historical Association for the Year 1893*, 199–227.

Tyler, P. A., Rice, A. L. and Young, C. M. (2001) Deep-sea biology in the 1990s: a legacy of the *Challenger* expedition. In M. Deacon, T. Rice and C. Summerhayes (eds) *Understanding the Oceans*. Routledge, London and New York, pp. 261–71.

US Department of Defense (2014) *Quadrennial Defense, Review*. Accessed at *http://www.defense.gov/home/features/2014/0314_sdr/qdr.aspx*.

Vallega, A. (1992) *Sea Management: A Theoretical Approach*. Elsevier Applied Science, London.

Vallega, A. (2001) *Sustainable Ocean Governance: A Geographical Perspective*. Routledge, London and New York.

Vukas, B. (2006) State practice in the aftermath of the UN Convention on the Law of the Sea: the Exclusive Economic Zone and the Mediterranean Sea. In A. Strati, M. Gavouneli and N. Skourtos (eds) *Unresolved Issues and New Challenges to the Law of the Sea: Time Before and Time After*. Martinus Nijhoff Publishers, Leiden, pp. 251–8.

Wagner, D., Tupaz, E. and Pozon, I. P. (2012) China, the Philippines, and the Scarborough Shoal. *The World Post*, 20 July. Accessed at *http://www.huffingtonpost.com/daniel-wagner/china-the-philippines-and_b_1531623.html*.

Wang, Z. and Zhang, J. (2010) China and the International Geophysical Year. In R. D. Launius, J. R. Fleming and D. H. DeVorkin (eds) *Globalizing Polar Science: Considering the International Polar and Geophysical Years*. Palgrave Macmillan, New York, pp. 143–55.

Warren, J. (2014) Actor Leonardo DiCaprio tells State Department conference the oceans need new protections to save them. *New*

York Daily News, 17 June. Accessed at *http://www.nydailynews. com/news/politics/leonardo-dicaprio-tells-state-department-conference-oceans-new-protections-article-1.1832624.*

Wenk, Edward, Jr (1972) *The Politics of the Ocean.* University of Washington Press, Seattle and London.

Wente, M. (2012) The agony of David Suzuki. *Globe & Mail,* 14 April, p. F9.

White, R. (1997) When Frederick Jackson Turner and Buffalo Bill both played Chicago in 1893. In R. C. Ritchie and P. A. Hutton (eds) *Frontier and Region: Essays in Honor of Martin Ridge.* The Huntington Library Press/University of New Mexico Press, San Marino, CA/Albuquerque, NM, pp. 201–12.

White House (2014) Fact Sheet: President Obama to designate largest marine monument in the world off-limits to development. Office of the Press Secretary, 24 September. Accessed at *http:// www.whitehouse.gov/the-press-office/2014/09/24/fact-sheet-president-obama-designate-largest-marine-monument-world-limit.*

Woo, E. (1999) Arvid Pardo; former UN diplomat from Malta. *Los Angeles Times,* 18 July. Accessed at *http://articles.latimes. com/1999/jul/18/local/me-57228.*

World Commission on Environment and Development (1987) *Our Common Future.* Oxford University Press, Oxford.

Yeats, C. (2012) Deep sea mining: exploration is inevitable. *SciDev. Net,* 7 November. Accessed at *http://www.scidev.net/global/earth-science/opinion/deep-sea-mining-exploration-is-inevitable.html.*

Zabarenko, D. (2011) Scientists tout deep oceans as hiding spot of 'missing' heat. *Globe & Mail,* 20 September, p. A17.

Zimmer, C. (2015) Vast study says stress on ocean life unprecedented. *Globe & Mail,* 17 January, p. A5.

Zolberg, A. R. (1994) Changing sovereignty games and international migration. *Indiana Journal of Global Legal Studies* 2(1), 153–70.

Index